THE ART OF TIME

TERESA PÉREZ HIGUERA

THE ART OF TIME:

MEDIEVAL CALENDARS AND THE ZODIAC

WEIDENFELD & NICOLSON
LONDON

Originally published in Spain by Ediciones Encuentro S.A. in 1997

First published in Great Britain in 1998
by Weidenfeld & Nicolson

Picture credits
Österreichische National Bibliothek, Vienna: 12, 145
Bibliothek National, Berlin: 15, 21-25, 112, 119, 139, 145
Cabildo de la Catedral de Gerona. Photographs by Domi Mora: 13, 14, 104, 105, 135
Imagen Mas: 27-31, 91, 93-95, 112, 127, 147, 156, 160, 161, 164, 169, 174, 190
Württembergische Landesbibliothek, Stuttgart: 17, 33-37, 101
Anotonio Pareja: 63-67, 109, 137, 148, 156, 170, 202, 217, 225, 237
Oronoz: 130, 131
Scala, Florence: 39-43, 96, 97, 103, 115, 121-123, 151, 155, 163, 175, 178-181, 183, 187, 193-195, 203-205, 207
Cabildo de la Catedral de Tarragona. Photographs by Domi Mora: 149, 159, 172, 173
Giraudon, Paris: 68, 69, 110, 189, 219, 252, 253
Sahats, editorial services: 45-49, 146, 158, 185
The British Library, London: 57-61, 80, 81, 86, 112, 133, 143, 153, 167, 175
Biblioteca Nacional, Madrid: 77, 82, 84, 85, 89, 141, 150, 157, 162, 165, 171, 188
Bibliotèque Nationale de France, Paris. Faksimile Verlag, Lucerne: 51-55, 73, 75, 83, 88, 177, 191, 197, 199, 208, 209, 211, 212, 215
Aurea de la Morena: 18, 19, 119

All photographs not listed above are from the archive of Ediciones Encuentro, S.A.

A CIP catalogue record for this book is available from the British Library
ISBN 0–297–82370–1

Weidenfeld & Nicolson

The Orion Publishing Group Ltd
Orion House
5 Upper Saint Martin's Lane
London WC2H 9EA

CONTENTS

For Tina

MEDIEVAL CALENDARS

To be able to measure time – the passing of the hours, days, months, seasons and years – by means of astronomy has been of vital importance to man ever since the beginnings of agriculture. Through observation of the phases of the moon, the movements of the sun, the solstices and the equinoxes, man was able to establish a timetable for crop production, the economic basis of the first agrarian societies, and so the calendar and agriculture have been inextricably linked from the earliest times. The months and seasons were represented in Roman art by means of allegories based on the different agricultural tasks, personifications that were general in decorative schemes, wall-paintings and mosaics and, above all, in illustrated calendars now lost to us; we have, however, a seventeenth-century copy of one of these, the *Chronograph of Philocalus of 354*, which contains early versions of much of the later iconography.

Vienna Calendar

These personifications continued in use into the Middle Ages, and in some examples from Carolingian and Ottonian times we can see how the ancient allegories were gradually replaced by images that more directly represent a particular agricultural activity, the point of departure for the calendars of Romanesque and Gothic times.

In the example known as the *Vienna Calendar* (Österreichische National-bibliothek), which dates to the year 837, the twelve months are identified by inscriptions. The inheritance of antiquity can be seen in the attributes, clothing and attitudes of the various figures. Some are difficult to interpret today – the swan of February, for example, and the snake of March, the same iconography as in the *Chronograph of 354*; these attributes appear again in the Gerona Creation Tapestry, from around the year 1100, where the figure corresponding to March grasps a snake and has a swan at his side, confirmed by the label 'CICONIA'. However, most of the months show the activities that will be the norm in medieval calendars too: ploughing in June, a man with a scythe about to cut the hay in July, reaping the wheat in August, sowing seed in September, a grape-picking and wine-making scene in October, while November and December share the traditional scene of killing the pig. For January, it has the traditional subject for the cold months, a man (unusually here a young man) warming himself at a fire.

A little more than a century later, from about 975, we have another calendar from the monastery of Fulda (Berlin, Bibliothek National). This calendar, from a time when the iconography was changing, includes two cycles: on one side, the depiction of the months showing a clear preference for agricultural tasks; on the other, an echo of classical motifs in the figure representing the Year in the centre, accompanied by personifications of Day and Night and the four Seasons. The inscriptions contain a fragment of the *Versus de anno et mensibus* attributed to Priscian.

This allegorical representation of the Year derives from a common Roman type in which the Year, often identified, as in the Fulda Calendar by the inscription 'Annus', occupies the centre (*annulus*) of a circle and is surrounded by different elements of the cosmology: the four winds, the signs of the Zodiac, and representations of the twelve months, to which are added, always in strict symmetry, the sun and moon, day and night, personifications of the Dawn, Midday, Afternoon and Night, and of the four seasons: Spring, Summer, Autumn and Winter. An example is the *Astrological Calendar and Mar-*

Gerona Creation Tapestry

tyrology of Swabia (Stuttgart, Württembergische Landesbibliothek), dated 1180. The imagery of the wheel of the year, with its classical references, is the origin of medieval versions of the theme, such as the floor mosaics of the cathedral of Aosta or of San Michele in Pavia, where the zodiac takes the place of the labours of the months. Most importantly, the figure of Christ now takes the place of the Year at the centre; he is shown as Sol de Justitia (the Sun of Justice), who governs the course of time, marking the passing of the months and the seasons.

An exceptional example of this is the Gerona Tapestry, dated about 1100. In the centre the Pantocrator presides over the universe, represented by Creation scenes from Genesis and by the four winds; surrounding it is a border, partly lost, with the figure of the year (ANNUS) above, in the middle and within a circle, and in the remaining compartments the four Rivers of Paradise, the Sun and Moon in their chariots, the four Seasons, and the twelve Months, which frame the central figure of Christ in his role as Lord of Creation and Lord of Time.

Gerona Creation Tapestry

Nevertheless, the circular composition, in the style of a planisphere, which beautifully expresses the concept of time as a cycle, was difficult to retain when, from the twelfth century on, calendars began to be used for the decoration of religious buildings. At first an attempt was made to adapt the circular calendar to the semicircular shape of the arched portals, but this was soon abandoned. In France, Italy and to a lesser degree Spain, the months were depicted in the form of seasonal agricultural tasks, not only in monasteries and cathedrals, but also in many rural churches; this no doubt led to the images being enriched with variations – details of local ways of working or of the different seasonal rhythms imposed by the different geographical regions. The examples that have been preserved give a sequence from the beginning of the twelfth century – with two very early examples in the Pantheon of San Isidoro de León and on the facade of Santa María de Ripoll – to the end of the thirteenth century, when calendars began to become less popular in churches, though there are still plenty to be found, in the capitals of

the cloisters of various cathedrals and monasteries, on the Fontana Maggiore in Perugia or in the decoration of the vault of Teruel Cathedral.

At the end of the fourteenth century the cycle of the months was taken up in a very different social context, which caused the nature of the images to be changed. The depictions of the twelfth and thirteenth centuries had preserved the ancient Roman tradition of 'personifications' of the months; even when the archetypal model was abandoned, the tradition of representing each month by a single figure (very occasionally accompanied by another) was respected. Then, in the last years of the fourteenth century and particularly in the fifteenth century, calendars came to be included at the beginning of Books of Hours and in other illuminated manuscripts, and, exceptionally, in the decoration of palaces such as the Torre Aquila in Trento or the Palazzo Schifanoia in Ferrara. The new court patronage brought about a change in the style, and the agricultural cycle now became more refined: the peasants appear to be nobles in fancy dress, not workers tired out by their labours; the single figure personifying the month gives way to a merry group in the midst of an idealized landscape, a stage backdrop. Moreover, the depictions of the months are frequently shown with the corresponding sign of the zodiac displaying the patron's culture and learning – though at times the interpretation of the signs is mistaken. The higher clergy now imitated the tastes of the nobility, including calendars among the miniatures of their de luxe missals and pontificals.

By the end of the fifteenth century, the style of calendars was changed again. Calendars illustrated by woodcuts or wood engravings were being printed for a wider audience, favouring a trend to more realistic scenes. A typical example is the *Grant Kalendrier compost des bergiers avecq leur astrologie et plusiers aultres choses*, printed en Troyes by Nicolas le Roge in 1495.

16

Swabian Calendar ➤

Abbey of St Denis, Paris ➤ ➤

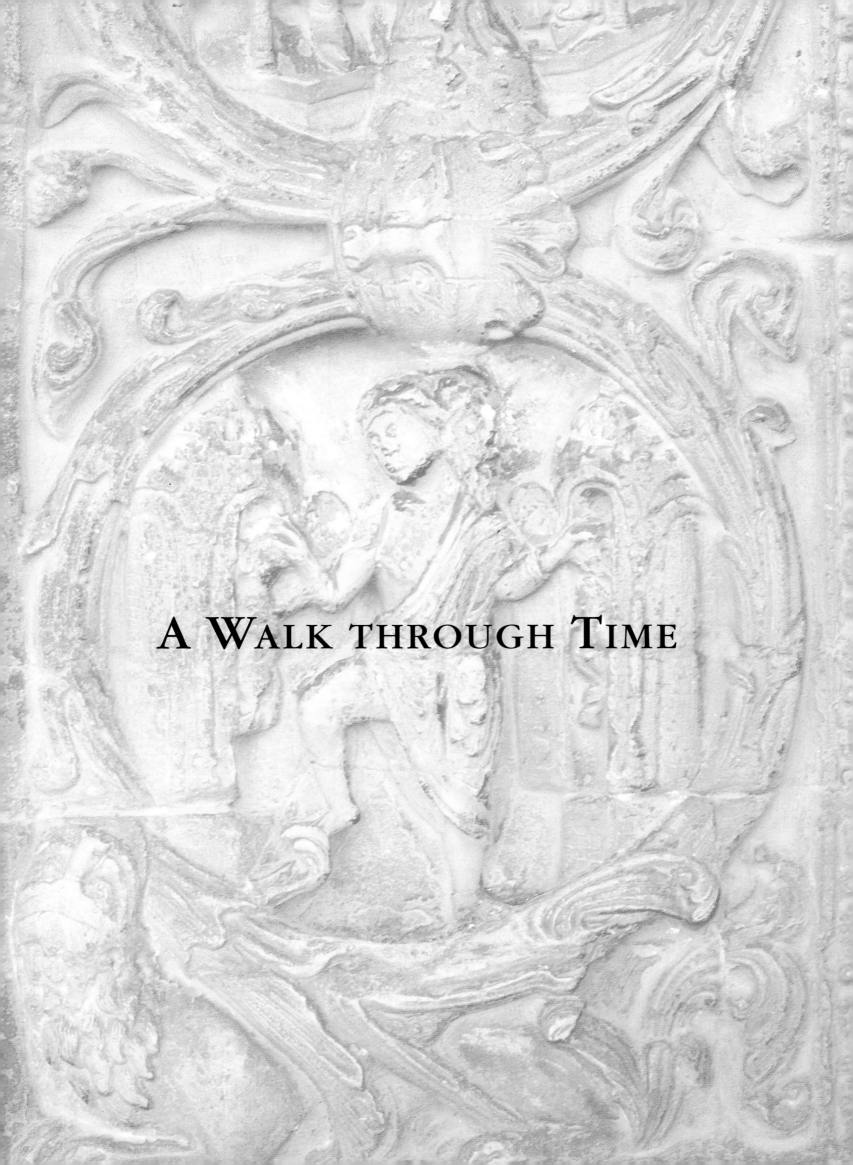

A Walk through Time

Fulda Calendar, c. 975
Berlin, Bibliothek National
ms. Theol. lat. 192

The months of the year, reading from top to bottom

22

SPRING

The month of May. The regeneration of the earth

A beardless youth seems to grow out of the earth between the two trees covered with green leaves that he clasps in his arms. The frontality of the figure recalls classical allegories of the seasons and indicates that he should be identified as the spirit of new growth.

SUMMER

The month of August. The fruits of the harvest

Once again the frontality and the attitude of the figure refers back to the classical tradition of allegory, in this case the figure of Summer, which has harvest fruits as its attributes.

23

AUTUMN

The month of November. Gathering firewood

At the end of autumn, after the new seed has been sown, firewood must be chopped and stored to provide warmth during the cold winter months. Here, the figure is clothed in tunic and cloak, showing its dependence on the iconography of calendar cycles of antiquity.

WINTER
The month of February. The beginning of the year's work on the land
Though it is still winter, it is necessary to start preparing the vineyards. Wearing a chlamys, which is quite inappropriate for this kind of work, he cuts away the dead stems of a vine.

León, San Isodoro, Panteon Real, frescoes
c. 1130

The months of the year, reading from top to bottom

SPRING

The month of April. The renewal of growth

The iconographic traditions of classical antiquity survived into the Middle Ages, particularly in depictions of the month of April: a young man, shown frontally, holds the branch of a tree in each hand.

SUMMER
The month of August. The harvest
After the reaping, the peasant threshes the grain with a flail, a
practice that survived until quite recently in some parts of Castille.
The flail he is using resembles the ancient Roman *pertica*.

AUTUMN

The month of October. Feeding the pigs

The last labour of the year is killing the pigs. First the animals have to be fattened up; so the peasant leads the herd to the woods where they can gorge themselves on the acorns that he shakes down from the oak trees.

WINTER
The month of February. The time of rest
After all the work has been done, the peasant warms his feet and hands at a good fire, staving off the winter's chill.

Astronomical Calendar and Martyrology of Swabai, c. 1180
Württembergische Landesbibliothek, Stuttgart
Cod. hist. 415

SPRING
The month of March. Fishing and pruning the vines
One peasant prunes a vine, the first of the year's agricultural tasks, while another holds a fishing fork and the fish he has caught. Even though fishing was one of the normal activities of medieval man, it is rarely shown in calendars, because it is not associated with a particular month.

SUMMER
The month of August. Reaping
Only the upper half of the figure is shown, because of the circular
format of the calendar, and no cornfield is shown. Nevertheless,
the peasant's task is easily identified: he is cutting the wheat with a
saw-toothed sickle. On the left-hand side of the picture the corn
has been tied into a sheaf.

35

AUTUMN

The month of September. Sowing

Having ploughed the field, the labourer then sows the seeds, scattering them with one hand, while with the other he holds up a cloth containing the rest of the seeds.

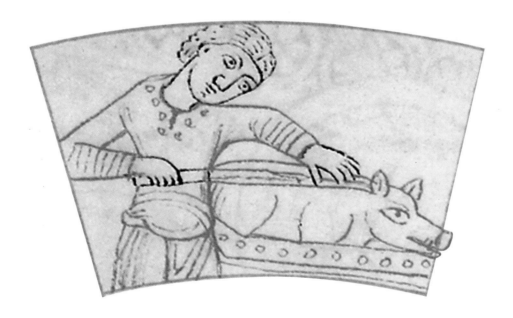

WINTER

The month of December. Killing the pigs

Here the artist has shown the moment immediately after the slaughter. The animal, on a plank or chopping block, is being quartered with a large knife.

Parma Baptistery, *c.* 1196, Benedetto Antelami

The months of the year, reading from left to right

SPRING

The month of April. The King of Spring
Sometimes the month of April is represented as the King of Spring,
a regal figure wearing a royal crown on his head, and holding a
branch like a sceptre in his right hand; while in his left hand is an
emblematic fleur-de-lis.

SUMMER
The month of August. Threshing
In some Mediterranean countries the grains of wheat were separated from the ears by oxen or horses trampling on the sheaves, which had been spread out over the threshing floor; the straw which was left was fed to the livestock.

41

AUTUMN

The month of September. The grape harvest

An important part of the legacy inherited by the Middle Ages from antiquity was a knowledge of astronomy and astrology; the signs of the Zodiac were sometimes included with the labours of the months in medieval calendars.

WINTER
The month of December. Other tasks
The phrase 'winter rest', as applied to the period from December to February, indicates only that there is no work in the fields during that time, for these are the months when the seed sown in November germinates. Gathering, chopping and storing firewood are, however, necessary for surviving the long cold winter.

Pamplona Cathedral, cloister bosses, first half
of the fourteenth century

The months of the year, reading from top to bottom

boss destroyed in
the nineteenth
century

SPRING

The month of May. May the knight

In the twelfth century there was a change in the traditional iconography of the month of May, from May the warrior to May the knight; the shield, symbol of the military spirit that characterizes this month in the classical tradition (for it was at the end of winter that new military campaigns were begun), is replaced by a falcon, the attribute of a knight.

SUMMER
The month of July. Reaping
The summer agricultural labour *par excellence* is the reaping of the wheat. The peasant normally cuts the stem halfway down so that the rest of the straw can be used as feed for the livestock or as kindling in winter.

47

48

AUTUMN
The month of September. Filling the barrels with wine
Transferring the wine from the vats to the casks requires great care
so that the work done in the preceding months is not wasted.

WINTER
The month of December. The nobleman's feast
The use of tablecloth, plates, goblets and utensils, and the
presence of several companions, indicates that this depicts a
nobleman's feast. This would become the standard subject for
illustrations of the months of December and/or January.

49

Les Très Riches Heures du Duc de Berry,
fifteenth century, Chantilly, Musée Condé

The months of the year, reading from left to right

SPRING

The month of March. Ploughing, pruning and sowing

The major advance in the agriculture of the Middle Ages was the replacement of the older system, in which fields were left fallow in alternate years by the three-field system. Each year the crops were rotated so that the land was left fallow for a year and was then planted with winter wheat; in the third year it would be planted with a spring cereal.

SUMMER
The month of July. Sheep shearing and reaping
Another of the peasant's tasks during the summer in the cooler parts of Europe, was the sheep-shearing: the sale of wool made an important contribution to the household economy.

AUTUMN

The month of September. The vintage

Grape picking is a co-operative task: the grapes are gathered into small baskets, which can be easily carried. They are then deposited in great wooden vats to be taken to the press.

WINTER
The month of December. The boar hunt
The boar hunt is one of the nobility's activities during December:
the huntsman calls with his horn to the knight, who will kill the
animal that the hounds have surrounded.

Bedford Hours, c. 1425
London, British Museum, ms. Add. 18850,
folios 1–12v.

The months of the year, reading from top to bottom

SPRING
The month of May. May the courtier
The personification of the month of May, as a knight with a falcon, was used in the fifteenth century to depict the countryside in spring. The horseman wears a green tunic appropriate to the courtly celebration of May day.

SUMMER

The month of June. Haymaking

In countries with a damp climate, the month of June is dedicated to the work of haymaking. The labourer is using a scythe with a long curved blade.

AUTUMN
The month of September. Trampling the grapes
The bunches of grapes are put in wooden vats where they can be trampled to extract the juice.

WINTER

The month of December. Killing the pig

The autumn sowing is the last of the agricultural labours of the year, but before the winter break the pig must be killed, to provide food for the family during the winter period.

61

Missal of the Archbishop Alonso Carrillo de Acuña, 1446-82, Toledo Cathedral, Chapter Library, ms. Res. 1

The months of the year, reading from top to bottom

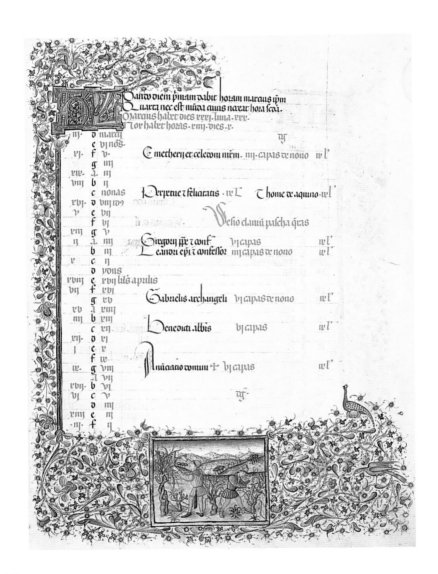

SPRING

The month of March. Pruning the vines

For the springtime pruning the medieval peasant in Mediterranean countries used the Roman pruning knife, the *falx vineatoria*, which had a wide, curved blade.

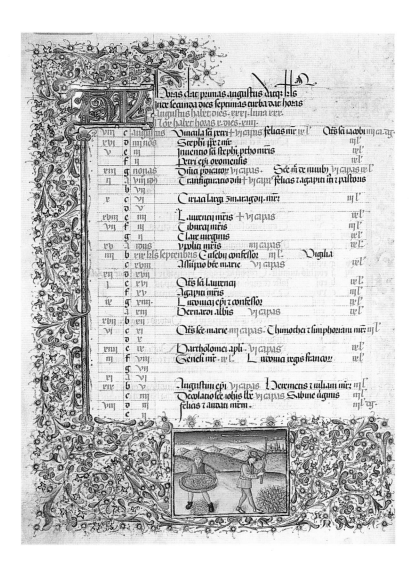

SUMMER

The month of August. The harvest

The Roman *pertica* becomes, in medieval illustrations, the flail that the peasant uses to thresh the wheat so as to separate out the grain. One person threshes the wheat and the other sieves it.

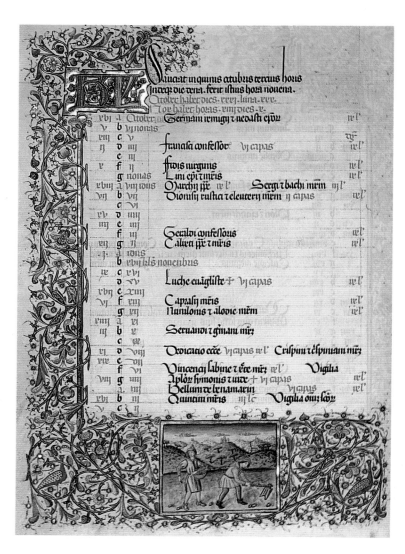

AUTUMN

The month of October. Sowing

After bringing in the harvest at the end of summer, the soil must be prepared for next year's crop. Ploughing and sowing close the annual cycle of cereal production.

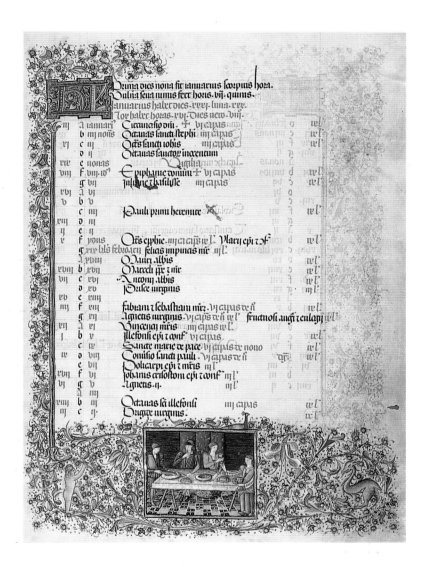

WINTER

The month of January. A nobleman's feast

In medieval banquet iconography, women are rarely shown, and only late in the fifteenth century are the servants shown: pages and women who serve the wine, carve the meat and cut the bread.

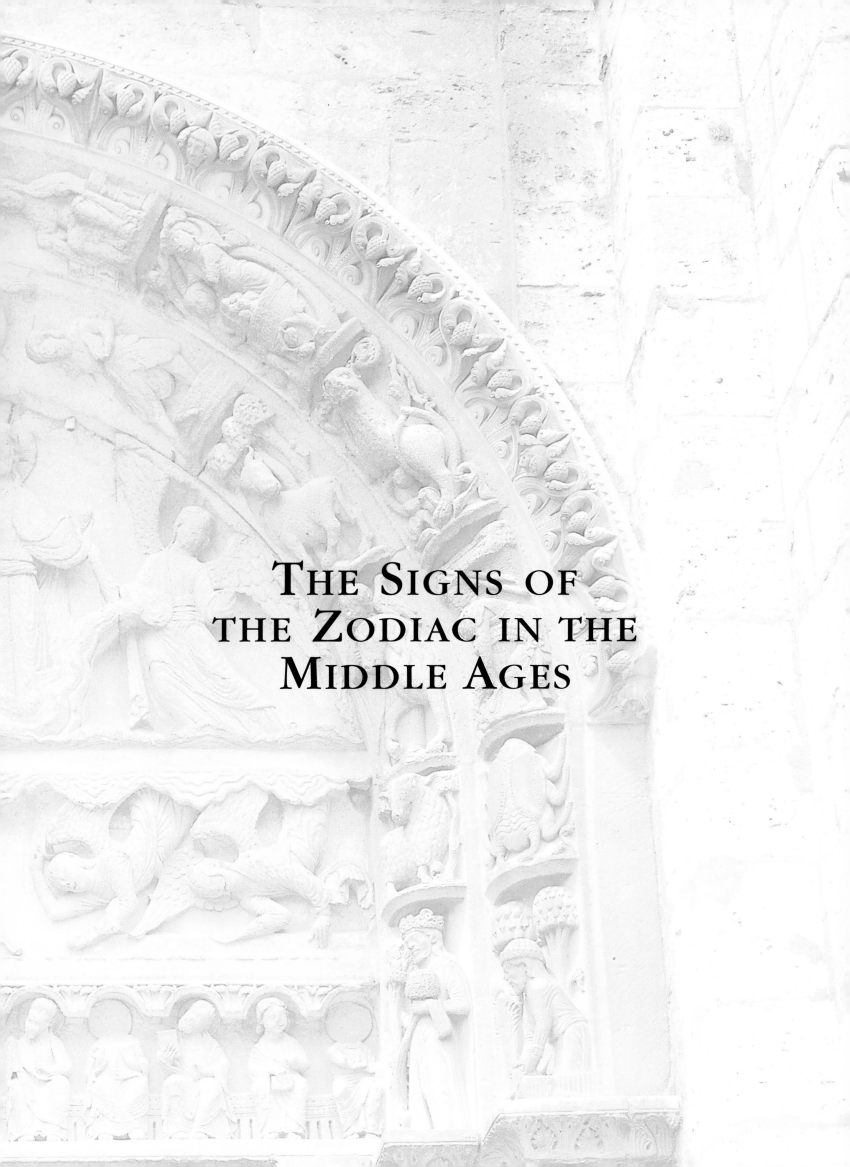

The Signs of
the Zodiac in the
Middle Ages

The Middle Ages inherited a considerable legacy of knowledge from antiquity, including a knowledge of the stars and the zodiac. The Chaldeans were the first to study the firmament – the most ancient depictions of some of the signs of the zodiac appear in the Babylonian 'kurrudus' – but it was the Greeks who established the definitive signs for the twelve constellations, images that, for them, evoked the arrangements of the stars in each of the constellations. Since the position of the sun changes relative to these constellations throughout the year, the twelve signs of the zodiac represent twelve periods of the annual cycle, and so came to be used as a calendar.

In the Middle Ages representations of the constellations themselves were confined to works of a scientific nature, but the signs of the zodiac were included in illustrated calendars, sometimes as an isolated theme, but more often in conjunction with personifications of the months. This linking of the two cycles – signs of the zodiac and representations of the months – gave rise to certain irregularities and errors. For example, month and zodiac sign are almost always shown as exactly equivalent, whereas in fact each month is associated with two signs, as is shown, exceptionally, in the calendar of the *Très Riches Heures du Duc de Berry* and the *Grant Kalendrier des bergiers*. Also, the year has to begin with Aquarius, because it is linked with January, whereas the zodiacal year begins with Aries, which marks the spring equinox; and Aries was in fact placed first in medieval texts on the subject.

Another probable consequence of the popularity of the signs of the zodiac in medieval calendars (a limited popularity compared with that of the depictions of the months) is the disappearance of the planispherical calendar, with the year at the centre of a large circle and the signs of the zodiac round the edge, as in the mosaic of Bet Alpha, of the sixth century, and in various manuscripts from the tenth to the twelfth centuries. However, the inclusion of the signs of the zodiac in the semicircular archivolts of cathedral doorways – as at Autun, the Madeleine of Vézelay or the Portail Royal at Chartres – may be interpreted as being derived from the circular calendars. In the thirteenth century the linear scheme becomes general; this works better when showing the two cycles in parallel, as in the socles and plinths of the facades of Gothic cathedrals, St Denis, Amiens, Notre Dame in Paris, Strasbourg, for example, yet it also appears in works where, like the *Breviari d'amor*, the illustrations accompany a text that refers solely to the zodiac. In this respect the calendar of the *Très Riches Heures du Duc de Berry* is exceptional: above the scene showing the occupation of the month is a blue semicircle with a starry background; in it is the Sun riding in its chariot – *auriga solis* – which advances from left to right, and the signs of the zodiac on the circumference in two unequal sectors, the smaller one on the left and the larger one on the right, towards which the sun's chariot is moving.

Finally, it is important to mention the continuity of the classical tradition in the iconography of the zodiac signs – unlike the representations of the labours of the months, which underwent many changes in the Middle Ages. It is true that, comparing different examples of zodiac signs from the Middle Ages, we see variations in the way in which they are represented, but these seem to arise in the usual way, from copies being made when the subject of the original is no longer properly understood – which occurs with all images inherited from classical times. In some cases, significant modifications take place; the most important are Aquarius being depicted as a woman, as in the *Breviari d'amor*, forgetting that its classical original is Ganymede; or, in the case of the Gemini, replacing Castor and Pollux by a pair of lovers, a formula that is

Les Très Riches Heures du Duc de Berry (detail)

repeated in numerous fifteenth-century manuscripts. It is evident that what we are dealing with here is a misinterpretation of the images rather than a conscious desire to modify them or substitute new ones. It must be remembered that there are many texts which have no illustrations and many illustrated texts in which the references to classical mythology are not explained. This can be seen when comparing the *Etymologies* of St Isidore with the text about the zodiac in the *Breviari d'amor*.

73

I. The Twelve Signs of the Zodiac

ARIES

According to St Isidore in the *Etymologies*:

> Aries, the first of the signs, is named thus, because of Jupiter Ammon, upon whose head sculptors depict ram's horns. The Gentiles established that, among the other signs, this one was the first, since according to them, the Sun begins its course in this sign in the month of March, which is the first month of the year.

Having forgotten the mythological relationship, the *Breviari d'amor* gives a new argument for justifying the image:

> The first sign is called Aries, which means ram, for the reason you will hear: just as the ram sleeps on both of his sides, sometimes on one side, and sometimes on the other, so also the sun, when it passes through this

Breviari d'amor

sign that is called the ram, is on both sides equal in relation to the earth, as much above as below and as much below as above. Its entry into this sign takes place on the twenty-fourth of March, and as the ways of this sign are equal, the days and nights are of equal length.

Despite this explanation, the illustration follows the normal model of a standing ram, in profile, facing left, with one foreleg slightly bent as if walking.

Since the illustrators would obviously have known the animal well, it generally appears quite naturalistic and, as a consequence, monotonous and repetitive. For this reason the miniature for the month of March in the *Bedford Hours* is surprising – its horns stick out at an unnatural angle on either side of its head. The explanation is given in the *Book of the Figures of the Fixed Stars* of Alfonso X, where it says that one of its horns points to the Septentrion (north), and the other towards midday (south).

TAURUS

As in the case of the ram (Aries), the medieval images of Taurus are clearly realistic and also give the profile view of the animal, with one or two of its legs bent to show that it is walking. Nevertheless, Taurus, in the *Book of the Fixed Stars* carries its head low, pawing the earth, and is cut in half with nothing from the waist down, since all the stars of this constellation are in the upper part of the body. This iconography, showing only the fore part of the animal, and as if charging, was used in the Hellenistic world and, beginning with Ptolomey's *Almagestus,* was transmitted to Arabic manuscripts, such as the *Catalogue of the Fixed Stars* of al-Sufi (Oxford, Bodleian Library), dated 1009–10. Exceptionally in the Christian world, the classical tradition survives in the Taurus of the zodiac on the Door of the Lamb at San Isidoro de León.

As regards the origin of its depiction as a bull, St Isidore considers it a homage to Jupiter, as in the case of Aries:

> In the same way they also include Taurus among the constellations, in honour of Jupiter, because according to mythology he turned himself into a bull when he kidnapped Europa.

The *Breviari d'amor,* on the other hand, seeks the reason in solar symbolism:

> The second sign is called Taurus, which means ox, because of these properties: just as the ox, in ploughing and passing over the land, makes it fertile and good and causes it to bear fruit, so also the sun, when it passes through this sign, warms the cold earth, and thereby makes things grow, multiply and bear fruit during this period, and does so quickly. It is also called Taurus because just as the bull is stronger than the ram, so the sun is stronger and more vigorous than when it runs through the sign of Aries or the ram, which is where the sun passes before going through the sign of Taurus.

GEMINI

As always, St Isidore refers to the mythological interpretation in order to justify the depiction:

> Castor and Pollux were placed after their death among the most well-known constellations. This sign has the name Gemini (the Twins).

The same identification will be repeated in the medieval texts, though they may seek a symbolic intention, as in the *Setenario* of Alfonso X, where it is argued that the figure showing two people who are inseparable is a symbol of Christ, who was similarly united to the Father. The usual references to the sun may also be added, as in the *Breviari d'amor*.

> The third sign is called Gemini for this reason: according to the ancient chronicle, Castor and Pollux were two brothers of great strength and vigour; scholars compare them with that sign because when the sun passes through it, it is stronger and greater than at any other time of the year, and its strength makes the earth bear fruit.

Unlike the two previous signs, the iconography of this one has numerous variations. The version closest to its classical origin is that of two nude young men who, even on the cape of Henry II of 1020, are armed with swords; the inscription *Gemini Castor et Polux curiale divi* confirms their names. This type disappears in other medieval depictions; it reappears in the illustration of the *Breviari d'amor*, but misinterpreted: the two youths, now dressed and armed with swords and shields, prepare to fight each other. The most frequent model, following the classical tradition, is that of two young men, either nude or with capes or tunics and mantles, who are facing the front with their arms intertwined.

In an unusual variation, the Alfonsan manuscripts show two nude figures: in the *Lapidario* their identity is ambiguous because their

79

posture hides their sex, but they are undoubtedly female in the *Manoscritto astrologico vaticano*. As A. Dominguez has pointed out, the description of the sign of Gemini in the *Book of Fixed Stars* of Alfonso X is followed here. They must be:

> Drawn as two women standing as if they are about to walk...embracing in a strange embrace, for they do not embrace with their faces held close, but diagonally, with their arms linked as if they were talking to one another.

That the classical origin had been forgotten is also evident in a model that was to be very common in the fifteenth century, although there were also isolated examples earlier: in this type the Twins have been replaced by a couple consisting of a man and a woman. It is possible that we are dealing with another case of the iconographic contamination that was frequent in the Middle Ages, here easily explained by the con-

Bedford Hours

nection between the sign of Gemini and the month of May, regarded in the early Middle Ages as the month of love and often represented by a pair of lovers in the calendars. In some cases, as in the miniature of the *Très Riches Heures du Duc de Berry*, the figures are naked, but more often a shield hides the lower part of their bodies, as in the *Bedford Hours*, where once again there is a certain ambiguity in the figures.

CANCER

St Isidore does not give any mythological origins for this sign, limiting himself to pointing out that:

> The name Cancer (Crab) comes from the fact that when the sun, in the month of June, arrives at this sign, it begins to recede as a crab does, and the days begin to be shorter. This animal has few markings on its forward part, and goes now to one side, now to the other, so that the forward part becomes the rear, and the rear becomes the front.

Bedford Hours

The *Breviari d'amor* repeats and corroborates this explanation: 'This is what St Isidore says and approves.'
In the medieval representations Cancer may be shown either as a crayfish or a crab; it is impossible to establish historical reasons, or the dependence on certain iconographic models, for the choice of one or the other. The crab, which appears in the *St G'all Aratus*, around the year 837, on the Door of the Lamb of San Isidoro de León, on the cathedral of Amiens, in the *Lapidario* of Alfonso X, in the *Très Riches Heures du Duc de Berry*, the *Breviari d'amor*, and the *Grant Kalendrier des bergiers*, is always shown from above, the sole variation being in the number of legs. On the other hand, the crayfish comes in several forms, sometimes appearing similar to the sign of Scorpio; it may be shown from above (as in the *Bedford Hours*), or from the side.

LEO

Once again St Isidore seeks the explanation for the sign in mythology:

> In Greece Hercules killed an enormous lion, and because of his valour it was included among the twelve signs (Leo). When the sun reaches this sign, it releases its enormous warmth on the world and causes the annual summer winds to blow.

Breviari d'amor

The *Breviari d'amor* takes up the reference to the sun:

> The fifth sign is named Leo because just as the lion is stronger and more vigorous than all the other animals, so also the sun, when it enters this sign, gives us greater strength and vigour through its heat, and its rays seem stronger and more burning to us, since at that time we are perpendicular to the sun.

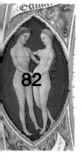

Again the iconographic variations are limited to different postures of the lion: in profile, walking towards the right or the left, and, exceptionally, seated, as in the calendar of the *Bedford Hours*, accentuating the parallel with heraldic beasts. The lack of first-hand knowledge of lions explains the 'humanoid' appearance of the animal in medieval depictions.

VIRGO

They also placed the sign of Virgo among the constellations, because in the times in which the sun passes through it, the earth, scorched by the heat, produces nothing. This is the period of the 'dog days'.

This is what St Isidore says about this sign, repeated by the *Breviari d'amor*.

The sixth sign is called Virgo because just as a virgin gives no fruit, so the sun, when it passes through and runs after this sign, absorbs the earth's moisture in its heat. In this way it takes away the earth's power to bear fruit.

Both texts contrast with the usual depictions of the sign in medieval calendars, which obviously depend on the personifications of the months. Virgo appears as a richly dressed woman who holds branches with fruit in her hands (on the Door of the Lamb of San Isidoro de León), palm branches (*Très Riches Heures du Duc de Berry*) and even a sheaf of wheat (various Books of Hours of the fifteenth century and the *Grant Kalendrier des bergiers*). In all these, the reference to a dry earth that produces no fruit has been forgotten, being replaced by an image that is close to the allegory

Les Très Riches Heures du Duc de Berry

of spring (tree branches with fruit) or summer (sheaves of wheat).

Another nuance can be seen in the case of the palm branches, which according to Christian iconography are the attributes of virgins and martyrs; this relationship is affirmed in the illustration of the *Breviari d'amor*, where a female figure with a crown and seated on a throne can be identified as the Virgin Mary. This explains her gesture, pointing to a vase with three flowering branches, for this is the well-known symbol of the virginity of Mary in the scenes of the Annunciation.

83

LIBRA

Breviari d'amor

According to the *Etymologies* of St Isidore:

> They gave the name Libra to this sign because of the equal balance of the month, since on the eighth day before the Kalends of October, the sun, traversing this sign, reaches the equinox. Hence Lucan says: 'according to the weights of the exact balance'.

This figure – holding a scale with the two pans more or less on the same level – appears in various depictions, such as the *Astrological Calendar and Martyrology of Swabia* of 1180, or the *Lapidario* of Alfonso X, or the *Très Riches Heures du Duc de Berry*; it is generally a woman who holds the scales. Her posture, standing and wearing a long dress, is very similar to that of Virgo, as can be seen in the representations of the cathedral of Amiens, the *Breviari d'amor*, the *Bedford Hours*, the *Grant Kalendrier des bergiers...*

SCORPIO

Here St Isidore says only:

> They designated Scorpio and Sagittarius thus due to the sun's rays that are proper to that season.

The *Breviari d'amor* expands on this:

> The eighth sign is the Scorpion. It has this name because, just as the scorpion is strong, poisonous and very dangerous, so also when the sun begins to descend and runs through this sign, the air also descends and passes through it, and since it does not get enough warmth from the sun for us who are below, it causes us harm and injury, as if it were a scorpion.

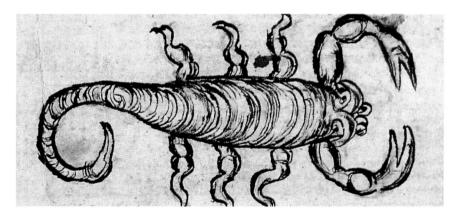

Breviari d'amor

That is, having forgotten the origin of this sign in the arrangement of the stars in the constellation – its eastern edge makes a curve with seven bright stars in it that to the ancients looked like the tail and sting of a scorpion – the medieval texts emphasize the dangerous (poisonous) nature of its tail. This is why the scorpion appears in bestiaries as a satanic animal, with fantastic characteristics and frequent errors in its depiction. The range of different images means that we can only describe for this sign very general scorpion-type whose common elements are confined to the long, articulated tail and the forward pincers or claws.

SAGITTARIUS

This sign illustrates particularly well the survival of the classical tradition. St Isidore describes it thus:

> Sagittarius has the figure of a centaur with deformed legs; they give him a bow and arrow to indicate the rays that belong to that month. Hence his name Sagittarius.

And that is how he is normally shown – as a classical centaur that has the top part of a man, naked to the waist, and the four legs of a horse. In the illustration of the *Breviari d'amor*, the equine part consists only of the hindquarters, giving a totally unstable air to the figure, which is supported by only two legs; it resembles another monster defined by St Isidore himself as the 'hippopod'. The miniature in the *Bedford Hours* is quite unusual, for the centaur is dressed in an elegant jacket with wide, lined sleeves and a hat, in the international Gothic style.

86

Bedford Hours

CAPRICORN

This is the sign whose iconography varies most. The images have in common the head and horns of a goat, referring to the constellation, and can be divided into three categories: those with the front part of a goat and a fish's tail, those with the front part of a goat emerging from the shell of a snail, and, rather rare, those that show a whole goat.

The first type is the one described by St Isidore in his *Etymologies*:

> They incorporated the figure of Capricorn in the constellation in honour of the goat that gave suck to Jupiter. They gave the hind part of her body the figure of a fish, in order to indicate the rains which often occur in the last days of the month.

The *Breviari d'amor* illustrates this type, but seeks a new explanation:

> The tenth sign is Capricorn, and it is named thus for this reason: just as the goat anxiously seeks the other goats, so also the sun, when it has sunk to this sign of Capricorn and cannot descend any more, immediately begins to return upwards, always returning through the other signs to the place it began, and begins to seek all the other signs. The sign of Capricorn has the figure of a fish from the waist down because towards the end of this sign rains must appear.

The same iconography, the top portion of a goat and a fish's tail, is also given in the *Lapidario* of Alfonso X and in the relief on the cathedral of Amiens. The second type, the top portion of a goat emerging from a snail shell, is widespread in the fifteenth century, in the calendars of Books of Hours, such as the *Très Riches Heures du Duc de Berry*, or the *Bedford Hours*. The third version, showing the whole goat is rather rare, but it can be seen in works as widely separated in time as the *Astrological Calendar and Martyrology of Swabia* of 1180, and the *Grant Kalendrier des bergiers* of 1495.

AQUARIUS

In the classical world, this sign was identified with Ganymede, the cup-bearer of the gods; one of the most frequent interpretations in the medieval world shows the figure of a young man emptying a jug. There are examples of this from the mosaic of Bet Alpha in the sixth century, right up to the fif-teenth century, in the *Très Riches Heures du Duc de Berry*, the

Les Très Riches Heures du Duc de Berry

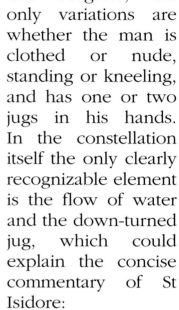

Bedford Hours, and the *Grant Kalendrier des bergiers*; the only variations are whether the man is clothed or nude, standing or kneeling, and has one or two jugs in his hands. In the constellation itself the only clearly recognizable element is the flow of water and the down-turned jug, which could explain the concise commentary of St Isidore:

They gave the names Aquarius and Pisces to them on account of the raininess of this time of the year, given that winter, when the sun traverses these signs, is when the greatest downpours are unleashed.

The *Breviari d'amor* repeats this, adding:

That is why it has the name Aquarius, meaning water.

This reference to water alone, the connection with Ganymede forgotten, may explain the illustration that accompanies the text in the *Breviari d'amor*: an undoubtedly female figure holding a bottle in each hand, and pouring water from the right-hand one.

PISCES

In the *Book of the Fixed Stars* of Alfonso X, it is said that this figure is drawn as if the two fish were tied together on a string, and this is the type that almost always appears in medieval depictions. The text adds that in the sky one is in the north and the other in the south, which explains the usual arrangement: parallel to one another with their heads facing in opposite directions. As with many other signs, the image in the *Breviari d'amor* is different: the two fish form a St Andrew's cross, their heads facing in opposite directions, something the text briefly clarifies:

> The last sign is Pisces, which is to say fish...You know that there are two fish. For this reason the writers of the treatise say that this sign has double vigour and two parts: the first looks toward the west and the other towards the north.

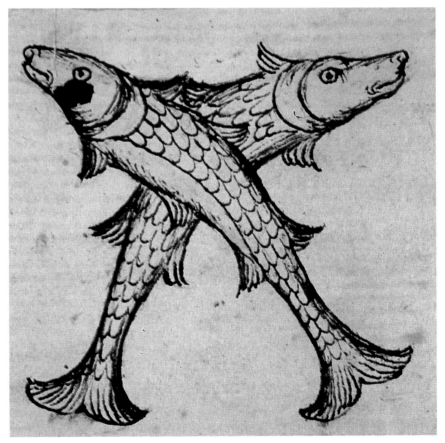

Breviari d'amor

San Isidoro de León, Door of the Lamb ➤

II. The Assimilation of the Zodiac by Christianity

In a religious era like the Middle Ages, in which the pagan feasts had from the very first been taken over and adapted by Christianity, it seems logical that the same process would operate in the case of the zodiac. The signs, because of their number, could be interpreted as symbols of the twelve prophets or the twelve apostles. At a deeper level, some Christian writers, in their sermons and commentaries, sought to establish a parallel between the signs of the zodiac and baptism: if man's birth and destiny is determined by the stars, then the rebirth symbolized by baptism releases the new Christian from this fate and marks the beginning of his or her new life under Christ's providence. This idea is expressed in a sermon by St Zeno, bishop of Verona between 362 and 371; the text has been signalled by S. Moralejo as a possible source for the interpretation of the zodiac which appears of the Door of the Lamb at San Isidoro de León.

Several signs in this cycle differ from the traditional ones, as was pointed out some years ago by Rada y Delgado, who suggested possible

San Isidoro de León, Door of the Lamb

San Isidoro de León, Door of the Lamb

Christian interpretations for some of the signs: Aries as the 'Agnus Dei', Virgo as the Virgin Mary, Gemini as two of the blessed – possibly the brothers Facundus and Primitivus, who were martyred at León under Marcus Aurelius – Libra as the incarnation of Justice, and more general allusions such as a reference to the Water of Life in Aquarius or to the symbol of Christ (a fish) in Pisces; he also noted that Capricorn and Sagittarius could represent the devil.

Basing his argument on the text of St Zeno, S. Moralejo has interpreted the reliefs at San Isidoro as an attempt to use the twelve signs of the zodiac to express the rebirth of the neophyte who has been introduced into an order where God's grace takes over from fate. Thus for Aquarius a figure pours water over two fish, an allusion to those who are newly united through baptism by Jesus Christ, '*noster Aquarius*', our Aquarius; the image connects also with Pisces, where a man in a boat appears behind the two fish, an allusion to the new Christians who will be caught by the '*piscatores*

93

hominum', the fishers of men – the apostles or their successors. Throughout his or her lifetime, the Christian must avoid and flee from sins such as avarice, represented by Cancer according to an astrological tradition which says that Cancer presides over the birth of avaricious businessmen and unscrupulous speculators; man is tempted by the devil himself in the shape of Sagittarius or Capricorn, representing adultery and lust, sins that in the Middle Ages were symbolized by the male goat. The Christian must overcome temptation, as St Luke says (x, 19):

'Behold, I give you power to tread on serpents and scorpions',

a verse quoted by St Zeno of Verona with reference to Scorpio. The Christian will overcome these with the help of the two Testaments, the book held up by the two figures with haloes, representing Gemini, and above all with the help of Christ himself, alluded to in Aries (Agnus Dei) and also in

San Isidoro de León, Door of the Lamb

Taurus, shown in a sacrificial scene, and Leo, the Lion of Judah – symbols of the passion and death of Christ, according to St Zeno.

The interpretation of the zodiac of San Isidoro as a representation of the baptismal liturgy is supported by the frequent association of the signs of the zodiac with baptism: on fonts, as at Grottaferrata, near Rome – where some of the reliefs closely resemble those of San Isidoro de León – at Brookland in Kent, at St-Evroux-de Montfort, and in Spain at Guardo, Palencia; or in baptisteries, such as Benedetto Antelami's reliefs at Parma or the floor mosaic of the baptistery in Florence.

San Isidoro de León, Door of the Lamb

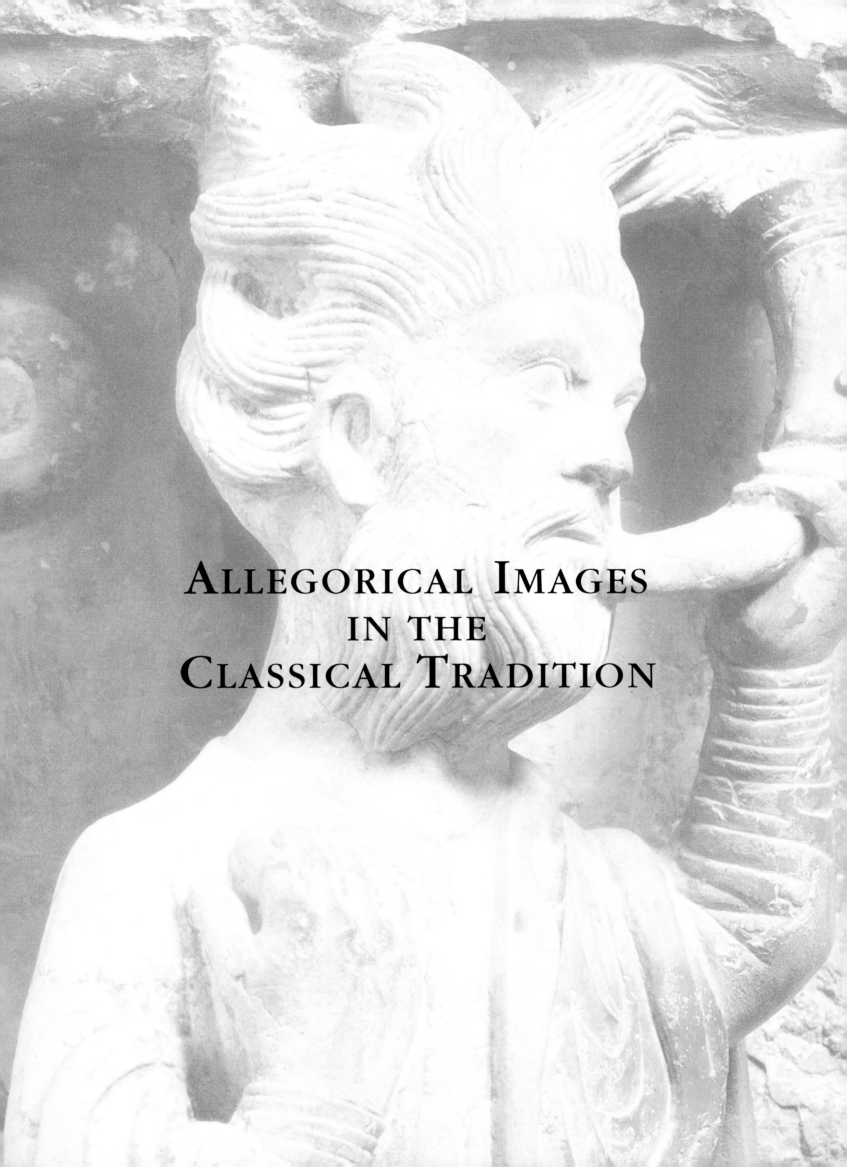

ALLEGORICAL IMAGES
IN THE
CLASSICAL TRADITION

In medieval calendars two quite different types of imagery can be distinguished. In the first, the more uncommon type, the allegorical nature of the images derived from antiquity is preserved and the figures have the conventional attributes established in Roman iconography. In the majority of cases, however, the frontal figures of classical allegory have been replaced by narrative scenes, but abstract personifications can still be found alongside the illustrations of everyday life which were generally preferred in the Middle Ages.

Nevertheless, the presence of figures derived from classical iconography is an important indication of the cultural inheritance of the Middle Ages and of the respect with which this inheritance was regarded by medieval man. In addition, the figures often show interesting changes in their iconography.

Autumnus

I. THE FOUR SEASONS

There are many examples of allegorical representations of the four seasons in Roman mosaics and paintings. Although some subjects, such as the personification of spring, also have precedents in the Greek world, it was in the Roman era that the iconographic models and their attributes were definitively established: spring with its flowers, summer with stalks of wheat and a sickle, autumn with bunches of grapes and vine leaves, and winter as an old man wrapped up against the cold. This image appears in Hesiod, who describes winter as an old man, frozen stiff. The theme was soon assimilated by Christian iconography and there are representations of the four seasons in the catacombs of Domitilla and of Praetextatus in Rome, and in the crypt of San Gennaro in Naples. The cycle of the seasons almost disappears in the Middle Ages, when calendars showing the labours of the months became popular. The classical personifications of the seasons now became the point of departure for representations of the months: winter for January or February, spring for April or May, and autumn for the grape harvest in September or October.

Parma Baptistery

The image of Spring as a figure carrying flowers is undoubtedly one of the most widely used allegories. Though of Greek origin, and connected with the nymphs and goddesses of fertility, the prototype was established in the Roman era as the personification of Flora, who is crowned with flowers and carries more flowers in a basket or holds them in her hands. This tradition is faithfully reproduced in the figure of April in the reliefs on the Fontana Maggiore in Perugia, dating from 1278, where she is wearing a classical tunic and cloak. In the slightly earlier figure by Benedetto Antelami on Parma baptistery, from the end of the twelfth century, she is depicted as a lady wearing fashionable contemporary dress, her mantle fastened by a brooch, though she still has the traditional attributes – the crown of flowers and a branch, now lost, in her hand. Thus the classical personification must be the origin of the representation of April as the Maid of Spring which appears in the calendars of the twelfth and thirteenth centuries.

The survival of classical tradition can also be seen in the depiction of winter as an old man well wrapped up in tunic and cloak. W. Endrei has drawn attention to the widespread diffusion of this image, beginning with Roman calendars, such as the *Chronograph of 354*, where it appears

Gerona Creation Tapestry

Gerona Creation Tapestry

as the personification of January. From the Carolingian era on, the hearth or fire for warming the hands also appears, as in the *Vienna Calendar* of 837 and the *Calendar of St Mesmin* of around the year 1000; the motif was later attached to February, the coldest month of the year. In Spain an important example showing the transformation of the iconography has survived in the Gerona Creation Tapestry, dated *c.*1100. An elderly or at least bearded man – his beard distinguishes him from the youths who represent the other seasons – warms his hands and feet at a fire, wrapped in a cloak and sheltering from the winds, which are shown as disembodied human heads identified by inscriptions, now lost, such as GELVS and FRIGVS ('icy' and 'cold'). Another inscription, of which little remains today, identifies the figure as HIEMS, or Winter.

The Gerona Tapestry also includes images of the other seasons (spring, summer and autumn) and of the months, being one of the few medieval calendars to include both cycles. The number 4 on the upper edge of the tapestry and the personification of the year in the centre, together with the inscriptions, confirms the identification of the cycle of the four seasons. This is of great importance because, apart from winter, the seasons do not follow the classical tradition: they are

105

represented not by personifications, but by figures of labourers carrying out seasonal agricultural tasks.

Spring is a young man working round a vine with a hoe, while in the upper left-hand corner a wind is depicted, in the form of a head with puffed-out cheeks. The figure of Spring is the prototype for the depiction of March in the cycles of the months as a peasant dressing and pruning the vines. Summer, clearly identified by the label ESTAS at the top, is again a peasant, this time holding in his left hand a sheaf of corn, the usual attribute of the classical figure of Summer. The scythe in his right hand – mistakenly labelled FLAX instead of FALX – however, derives from Carolingian models such as the depictions of July in the *Vienna Calendar*, the *Martyrology of Wandalbert of Prüm* or the *Fulda Calendar*, an image that reappears as a haymaker in later calendars. Autumn (AVTVNVS) is shown as a peasant gathering grapes, the usual image for September or October in the cycles of the labours of the months. The man prepares to cut a bunch of grapes with the sickle he holds in his hand.

Thus, in the cycle of the seasons in the Gerona Tapestry we see the beginning of the process that leads on to the calendars of the twelfth and thirteenth centuries: the replacement of the personifications derived from antiquity by narrative scenes of agricultural tasks.

106

II. April 'Floridus'

108

 This is an example of the opposite process: although the cycles of the months in the medieval calendars usually show the peasant carrying out his daily work, the iconography for the month of April frequently refers back to an image from late antiquity, as is shown by the hieratic attitude and the frontal pose. It must be related to the figure of Spring, in as much as it is the time of the rebirth of vegetation, yet in medieval calendars, as in antiquity, there are two different forms: the feminine one, the goddess of the flowers and cereal crops, the Maiden of Spring, and the masculine one, the Spirit of Vegetation.

The Maiden of Spring is the medieval version of the Roman goddess Flora, and like Flora she has garlands of roses and holds flowers in her hands as her attributes. She appears in the cycles of the months from the twelfth century on. She preserves the memory of her classical origins in her flowers, and also in her long robe and the frontal, symmetrical pose, with her hands raised to display the flowers she is holding. This is how she is shown in the oldest examples, as in the facade of the parish

Beleña de Sorbe

church at Beleña de Sorbe, near Guadalajara, or the paintings in the cathedral of Roda di Isábena, near Huesca. On the other hand, spring is commonly connected with May as well, and although the identity of April/Flora is always preserved, the image may have popular links with the traditions of May Day and the May Queen, still celebrated in many villages in Castille: a young boy or girl is chosen from the village, set on a dais and covered with flowers, as if he or she were a statue of Flora. The parallel is accentuated by the fact that some representations, such as that at Beleñade Sorbe, have a small pedestal below the feet of the figure, which could be interpreted as a remnant of the 'podium', or pedestal.

The other variant, the masculine one, has its origin in Robigus, the Roman god of mildew; the Robigalia was celebrated on 25 April with floral processions through the fields to propitiate the god and so promote a good harvest. As M.A. Castiñeiras has pointed out, the concept was used in calendars during the Carolingian period as the representation of April. In the *carmina* of Salzburg, of about 855-9, April is celebrated as bearing bunches of herbs and surrounded by vegetation, which explains the illustrations in the *Martyrology of Wandalbert of Prüm* and in the *St Mesmin Calendar* of a man with budding stems in his hair and hands. In the calendars of the twelfth century he is depicted as a youth, shown frontally, who holds the branch of a tree in each hand. In Spain, an early example is the APRILIS in the Pantheon of San Isidoro in León, though the model did not become widespread until the Gothic period, as in the portal of St Denis, the frescoes of Pritz (Mayenne), the altar frontal of Arteta and the illustrations of the *Breviari d'amor*, etc., in all of which the frontality inherited from antiquity is preserved. Moreover, in a cloister boss of the cathedral

109

of Pamplona the figure stands on a pedestal, as at Beleña.

The traces of this iconography persisted until the fifteenth century, though the stiff, hieratic style of the primitive model was abandoned. They are still present in the image of the peasant with a large branch (almost a small tree) on his shoulder who represents April in the *Bedford Hours*, and in the horseman crowned with flowers, also with a large branch on his shoulder, in the cloister of Santa María la Real in Nieva – though in this case the image represents the month of May. The great size of the branch which he holds could be an allusion to the maypole. Once more we have the cross-fertilization of images common in medieval iconography, which in this case goes back as far as the *Fulda Calendar* from the end of the tenth century: April, on foot and dressed in a tunic and chlamys (a Greek cloak), holds two flowering branches, and the plants on either side of him are also bursting into flower, whereas May, again a beardless youth, is an extraordinary image, for he appears to be growing from the ground, and he is clasping two budding trees, which spring from the same earth. Evidently April 'Floridus' has been taken over for the image for May, which is here represented by the Spirit of Vegetation. The same thing can

111

< Notre Dame de Pritz

ᐱ ᐱ Bedford Hours

ᐱ Fulda Calendar

ᐱ ᐱ Santa María de Nieva

ᐱ Fulda Calendar

be found in literature, when the *Libro de buen amor* defines April as:

full of flowers

whereas in the *Libro de Alexandre* it is May which is described as:

crowned with flowers

Finally, it should be pointed out that the representation of April as the King of Spring is a creation of the Middle Ages. On the relief from the Parma baptistery, by Benedetto Antelami, the figure wears a royal crown on his head and his whole bearing is regal: in his right hand he carries a branch as if it were a sceptre, and in his left is an emblematic fleur-de-lis. Even more striking is the figure – of May this time – on a capital in St Mark's in Venice, in which the king is seated on a throne and he is being crowned by two girls. A further example is the scene corresponding to April in a cloister boss in Tarragona, which Puig y Cadalfalch identifies as depicting the feudal rite 'in mixtio manuum': a youth, on his knees, offers a fleur-de-lis in homage to his lord, who is sitting on a throne.

Parma Baptistery ➤

III. Two-faced Janus

116

T his image is one of the most common in medieval calendars for representing the month of January. It is a typical example of the development in iconography which occurs in the medieval period. Its origins in Roman mythology are beyond doubt, but in the Middle Ages it is altered and reinterpreted, to such an extent that in the end the identity of the figure is forgotten. This can be shown from literary sources. First St Isodore, who explains the reasons for the image:

> The month of January (Ianuarius) takes its name from the god Janus, to whom the pagans consecrated it; or perhaps because this month is the threshold and door (*ianua*) of the year. For this reason too Janus is represented with two faces, so as to indicate that it is the entry and exit of the year.

This explanation is repeated in the *Primera cronica general* of Alfonso X:

> ... thus they named that month after Janus, who was an honourable and very mighty king, and they depicted him with two heads because he begins one year and ends another, and with one face he looks upon the things of the year that has passed and with the other on that which is to come.

However, the *Libro de Alexandre* gives a new iconography, connecting January with the winter feast:

> Don lanero was there, looking both ways,
> surrounded by roasted meat, carrying wood for the fire,
> he had large hens and was cooking them,
> he was at the grill, preparing sausages

an explanation that the *Libro de buen amor* repeats, though here the name is not mentioned:

> Following him was the two-headed one.
> Such a one looks in two directions,
> often eating well-seasoned game birds.

And then, the origin of the forgotten, January is described thus by Matfre Ermengaud in the *Breviari d'amor.*

> Know you that January is painted with two faces; and this is because at the entrance and exit of the year he looks two ways, that is, towards the autumn season and towards the winter season; and hence he is depicted with two faces.
> He is also represented as a man who enjoys eating and drinking, so as to show that at this time of year, because of the cold, interior warmth is more necessary for men's bodies, and for this reason more food is consumed and a man naturally wants more to eat.

117

The numerous variations on the imagery for January can be divided into four groups: 'Janus inter portas' and 'Janus claviger' from the classical tradition, and Janus at table or warming himself by the fire, as in the medieval reinterpretations of the theme. There are also a few atypical images, such as the Janus with a sword in the *Fulda Calendar*.

The figure of 'Janus inter portas' is the type closest to its Roman origins. Ianus was the first king of Latium, and was venerated as the god of peace. When Julius Caesar instituted the Julian calendar in 47 BC he dedicated the first month of the year to this god. From then on there are literary references to the two-faced image and to his function as janitor, or doorman, a function which, according to Ovid, he performed on Olympus. However, according to M.A. Castiñeiras, the motif of opening and closing of doors which often accompanies representations of January refers to the ceremonies performed in Rome at the temple dedicated to Janus; this would explain why classical architecture is often shown. This can be seen in the GENVARIVS in one of the earliest medieval calendars, the frescoes of the Pantheon at San Isidoro in León. The type was already fairly widespread throughout Europe; similar examples which are close in date can be found in the mosaics of the cathedral of Aosta, in northern Italy, and in the reliefs on the portal of St Denis in Paris. In the latter, dating from about 1140, the two faces of Janus are clearly differentiated: one belongs to an elderly man who has a long beard, while the other belongs to a young man, an allusion to the old and new years. This idea is reiterated in the two naked children that appear in the doorways on either side of Janus, one of them turning his back and leaving, the other entering – again representing the old and the new year. At San Isidoro and at Aosta the composition is simplified, showing only the two doors, one open and one shut.

'Ianus Clusivius' or 'Ianitor claviger', who holds up one or sometimes two keys, alluding to his role as doorman of the year, also has antecedents in classical literature. As with the 'Ianus inter portas', the motif was introduced at an early date in medieval calendars, although it became more widespread in the Gothic period; there are examples in the facade at Arteta and in one of the bosses in the cloister of Pamplona cathedral. In both cases January carries two enormous keys, which seem to be related to the two doors which appear in other versions; however, in the *Bedford Hours*, of the fifteenth century, the text refers to a single door opening on to all four seasons:

Fulda Calendar

Abbey of St Denis, Paris

As January holds the key to the year and opens the door to the four periods – spring, summer, autumn and winter – of which it is the beginning.

The miniature itself, however, shows January seated at a table eating and drinking with two of his faces, while a third face is added in the centre. This iconography of a three-headed Janus also appears on the facade at Arteta; it may have been adopted for reasons of symmetry, although it has also been suggested that it is a reference to the Trinity. It is an example of the way in which a new type can be formed once the original source has been forgotten. The same thing happens with the other two types – Janus at table and Janus warming himself at the fire – which have become assimilated with the images of the winter feast, the traditional scene for January or February, and that of the old man close to the fire, for February. This seems to have its origin in English calendars, where Janus is described as

he who drinks from cups,

an image which also appears in Chaucer's 'Franklin's Tale':

Janus sit by the fyr with double berd,
And drynketh of his bugle horn the wyn.

119

In the illustrated cycles both of these versions occur. The meal appears more often, and is linked to the popularity of scenes of the farm workers feasting after the day's labours – though in the case of Janus it is closer to the scene of the nobleman's feast, for the table is covered by a cloth and there are servants as well. There are plenty of allusions to the cycle of the agricultural year; the enormous hog's head, fruit of the previous month's labour, in the Pritz frescoes, is an example.

The image of Janus warming himself at the fire is less frequent. There is a very early example, around 1000, in the *St Mesmin Calendar*, but later it seems to be limited to certain Italian cycles, such as the floor mosaic at Bobbio or the relief on the western portal of Parma cathedral. There are two more Italian versions of the theme: at Borgo San Donnino (now Fidenza) Janus, as well as warming himself at the fire, is cooking himself a meal – which must be linked with the popularity of kitchen scenes in Italian calendars; a scene now in the cathedral museum at Ferrara – it comes from the south facade of the cathedral and is dated about 1240 – shows Janus seated, and holding a large jug, like the figure of Aquarius in the signs of the zodiac.

CALENDARS AND
MEDIEVAL SOCIETY

Thus the house of God that we believe to be one is threefold: in this world some pray, some fight, and some work; these three are united, and they cannot bear to be separated; on the function of the one the other two rely, each in his turn helping the others.

(Adalberon, Bishop of Laôn, d. 1031)

It has been shown that since its origins the human race has been divided into three: those who pray, those who work and those who fight; this proves that each is for the other the object of reciprocal care.

(Gerard, Bishop of Cambray,
Gesta episcoporum camaracensium **(1025),**
III, 52.)

I · THE PEASANT CALENDAR

As Le Goff has pointed out, the presence of the peasant in medieval calendars is inevitable, since agriculture dominated the era and the growing cycle regulated men's lives. Everyone, clerics, knights and peasants, depended on the land and the different tasks involved in the cultivation of the fields marked the annual rhythm. These are the images most often used in calendars to illustrate the months, and they are known collectively as 'the labours of the months'. This term is somewhat misleading, since the agricultural year comprises two rather different periods: one, from March to November, of continuous activity in the fields, when the tasks follow each other without interruption, and the other, a period of leisure and rest in winter and early spring. But J. Le Senecal's phrase 'occupations of the months' is also unsatisfactory, since it is equally inadequate as a description of feasts and leisure activities.

The connection between the iconography of the months and agricultural labours had been firmly established in Roman calendars, both the personification of the seasons and in the 'menologia rustica' that were widespread within the increasingly rural society of the late Empire. From this common tradition came both the Byzantine calendars in which the illustrations are faithful survivals of the images and archetypes of the ancient world, and also the western cycles, in which, as early as the Carolingian era, there are the beginnings of a process of transformation. This is a result of the new delight in nature and also of the preference for making the depictions into genre pictures, in which the peasant himself is shown carrying out the agricultural tasks.

It is possible that this link between field labours and the scenes of the months may help to explain the popularity of the calendar in the iconographic schemes of churches and cathedrals during the twelfth and thirteenth centuries. Also relevant is the great improvement in agriculture in Europe during those years. In addition, there is the hypothesis argued for some time by E. Mâle, and more recently by C. Frugoni. Both these authors point out that the Church glorifies work as a means of redemption: Christ has ransomed mankind, but each individual must merit this grace and so share in their own salvation. In the thirteenth century, Vincent de Beauvais teaches in his *Speculum doctrinale* that man can redeem himself from the Fall through 'science', a term that in the Middle Ages is equivalent to knowledge and work in all their forms. Thus work freely accepted is not seen as divine punishment, but rather as a means of redemption; it is the collaboration of man in the creative work of God. Of the various kinds of work, the cultivation of the land is the most important, for it was imposed on Adam, the first man, by God himself, according to the Genesis narrative.

In recent years, calendars have been studied for their contribution to sociology, as well as for the information they contain on farming systems and different aspects of medieval technology (a theme that was dealt with as early as 1940 by J. Caro Baroja in an article in which he gathers together, for the first time, the best-known Hispanic cycles. Today, the works of P. Mane on French and Italian calendars of the twelfth and  thirteenth centuries, of C. Frugoni in Italy, and on those of the Iberian peninsula by M. A. Castiñeiras, enable us to take a more general approach to the subject. Also, with the help of recent comparative

analyses, we can now pinpoint regional differences, due to small local variations in the time of the year when the different agricultural tasks were carried out and in the various techniques which were used. In Spain, as in most Mediterranean countries, agriculture is based on cereal cultivation, which involves ploughing and sowing, weeding and threshing; and on growing grapes, which involves pruning, harvesting and wine-making; to these may be added the raising and slaughter of pigs as a contribution to the peasant family's economy. Cycles depicting these activities were already well known by the beginning of the twelfth century; two important early examples are the frescoes in the Royal Pantheon of San Isidoro de León and the reliefs of the facade of Santa María at Ripoll. Throughout the twelfth, thirteenth and fourteenth centuries, the same cycles flourished, although from the middle of the thirteenth century there was a gradual decline in the numbers of cycles carved on churches and an increase in the use of calendars for illustrating manuscripts. The theme acquired a new vigour in the fifteenth century, when it was invariably included in missals and Books of Hours. However, the new patrons, the different techniques of manuscript painting and the artistic developments of the time brought about changes in the iconography, even in the scenes of agricultural labours.

132

1. The Labours of Spring

134

Once the winter was over, the peasant started again on his work in the fields. Ancient rites and celebrations of the arrival of spring and the renewal of the growing cycle were adapted to Christianity, usually focusing on promoting a good harvest; similarly, the iconography of the pagan world appears alongside depictions of the labours of the months, especially for April and May.

Some depictions record what is considered the most important development in the agricultural technology of the Middle Ages: instead of leaving fields fallow in alternate years, the new crop rotation meant that only a third of the land was left fallow in any one year; the rest was divided between winter cereals (wheat and rye), which had a long growing cycle and were planted in autumn, and spring crops (barley,

APRILIS

135

Gerona Creation Tapestry

oats and legumes), which were harvested in the same year. The land that was left fallow in the first year was sown with wheat in the winter (to be harvested the following summer) and with spring cereals or legumes in the third year, so as to achieve maximum productivity.

As a consequence, it now became necessary to plough in March and April for the spring cereals, and that is how April is represented in the Gerona Tapestry, dated around the year 1100; this is a good example of how up-to-date the calendars were with respect to the agricultural revolution of those years. A man – the figure had been lost and was recovered in the restoration of 1975 – guides a plough pulled by horses, which he prods with a goad. The plough, with wheels, and using horses rather than oxen, recalls central European types; also, a very similar example appears in the Bayeux Tapestry, woven between 1077 and 1088, and therefore only a few years earlier than the Gerona Tapestry. This type of plough was especially suited to damp terrain, and makes deep furrows in the earth, shown as thick black lines in the tapestry. It is probable that the location of Gerona near the French border explains the knowledge and use of what according to Pliny was a Gallo-Roman technique – and one that was unusual, except in Navarra and Vitoria, as Caro Baroja has pointed out.

This use of different types of crops, is the reason for the two depictions of reaping in the calendar of the Pantheon of San Isidoro de León. The same peasant prepares to cut the stalks with a sickle in June and July. Two scenes are labelled and the difference in the colour of the corn (lighter in June, golden in July) allows us to deduce that the first shows the barley harvest, a spring cereal, and the second wheat, a winter cereal. Although I know of no other example of the duplication of the scenes of reaping in medieval calendars, there is a parallel in the text of the *Libro de buen amor,* where June is described thus:

> ...he carries in his hand a scythe,
> and reaps the barley of all that domain.

Whereas in July:

> ...he carries the rye,
> wheat and all the corn to the threshing floor.

Beleña de Sorbe

And the same allusion to the different length of the crop cycles is made in designating March as:

the season in which the oats grow.

And the wheat and rye prosper

with the winds that April brings.

In the spring months some work was necessary on the long-cycle crops, though it is not normally shown in the calendars, since a single image was chosen to characterize each of the months. The weeding scene that appears on the facade of Beleña de Sorbe for June is therefore quite exceptional. (Weeding eliminated the thistles from the fields that had been sown, and so in Spanish it is called *escarda*, from the word for thistle, even though darnels, thorns, and other weeds were common as well.) Weeding normally took place in March and April, when the frosts were over and the time of the year favoured the germination of the wheat. Because weeding is an unlikely subject for June, I. Ruiz Montejo recently suggested that the Beleña scene should be interpreted as illustrating the custom of gathering herbs and flowers on the night of the feast of St John, which has its origin in the celebration of the summer solstice. It was believed that on the night of 23-24 July certain plants acquired magic healing properties and were able to ward off evil spells. Among those was the thistle, which was hung in doorways to prevent the entry of evil spirits, which would be caught by the thorns. But the peasant is shown in the midst of a field of ripe cereals, and is using a weeding hoe, a tool used to pull up the roots of the thistle, which seems to confirm the usual opinion that it really is a weeding scene, similar to the one depicted for June in the Fulda Calendar of about 975; there are other parallels in English calendars of the twelfth century described by J.C. Webster. P. Mane notes that weeding was carried out soon after St John's day, when the wheat is almost ripe, citing, as the sole example known from the twelfth and thirteenth centuries in France, the font of Saint-Evroult in Montfort, where the tool depicted is the same as that at Beleña.

Other tasks, such as the gathering of the early fruit, are frequently illustrated in Italian calendars, whereas in Spain they tend to be the

138

Fulda Calendar

exception. The scene for May at Santa María, Ripoll, a scheme derived from late antiquity, shows a man, aided by two youths, gathering fruit. The tree is identified by Puig i Caldafach as a cherry tree, mistakenly I believe, although its poor state of preservation makes it difficult to identify the species. The possibility is interesting, however, because of its literary connections. In the *Libro de Alexandre*, June is described as the month when

> … the cherry trees are loaded with ripe cherries.

And in the *Libro de buen amor* it says that:

> His hands are stained by all the cherries.

It is in fact the cherry harvest that is frequently shown in the Italian cycles.

Without a doubt, the task that characterizes spring, and virtually the only scene for March in the medieval calendars, is the pruning of the vines. The extensive cultivation of the vine in Mediterranean countries explains the large number of depictions in calendars

PRUNING

139

from Italy, France and Spain, for both spring and autumn; the illustrations often include interesting details of the techniques and tools used. In spring, in addition to pruning the vines, it was necessary to hoe round them in order to improve their growth, as well as to do any necessary grafting. According to the *Libro de buen amor*, these labours took up the month of February:

> ...what this month ordered was the pruning of the vines,
> to make good grafts, and to tie in the stalks;
> he ordered the planting of vines, so as to give good wine.

And March, that

> ...to the vines sent workers,
> so as to make many grafts, the good grafters.

Now although hoeing between the vines appears in some depictions, and characterizes spring itself in the Gerona Tapestry, the image of the peasant who prunes the vine predominates over all others for March. For this reason, the scene that appears on the relief in the cloister of the cathedral of Tarragona seems odd: it shows a person cutting off dead branches and another hoeing round the foot of a vine, as had been the practice in Spanish vineyards since Roman times, referred to by Columela and later by St Isidore. Pruning appears as early as *c.* 975 in the *Fulda Calendar* as an illustration for March; numerous examples from the twelfth century show the Roman pruning knife, the *falx vineatoria* described by Columela, a cutting tool with a curved blade for carrying out various operations: there is a hook on the end for removing unwanted shoots and a hatchet on the back of the blade for cutting off the dead branches. The blade might be curved like a small sickle (as in Roda de Isábena, the facade of Arteta, the frescoes of Pritz, the boss in the cloister of the cathedral of Pamplona or the illustration of the *Breviari d'amor*), or it might be straight, almost like a knife (Pantheon of San Isidoro de León, the facade of Beleña de Sorbe).

The depiction of the vines themselves is rather more varied: they are almost always reduced to a few branches, but sometimes they are more

imaginatively drawn: in the *Breviari d'amor* and in the cloister of Santa María la Real in Nieva they are trees with huge leaves; in the latter an early cluster of grapes is added; the use of stakes, as on the relief of the cloister of Tarragona, was exceptional.

2. Summer's Tasks

T his is the period of greatest activity for the peasant, who from June on, in the hottest months, must cut the hay, reap the wheat and then store the grain; in autumn comes the grape harvest and wine-making. This intense labour is reflected in the calendars, which never show anything other than farm-work for the months of June, July and August.

CUTTING THE HAY   June is dedicated to cutting the hay, a common scene in French calendars – less so in Spanish cycles, where it is sometimes replaced by the early gathering of wheat in the area of Catalonia, and also in Italy. Stern notes that hay-making was first shown in the area between the Loire and Belgium, and became widespread from the ninth century. The subject is easily identified by the scythe, which has a large curved blade – between 60 cm and 1 m – attached at a right angle to a shaft; there is normally a small handle on the lower part so as to make it easier to hold,

144

since it is manipulated with two hands. It appears in calendars from the Carolingian era on – for example in the *Vienna Calendar* and the *Fulda Calendar*, although here it is the illustration for July, whereas in the French examples of the twelfth and thirteenth centuries it corresponds to June.

The images show the peasants in different attitudes: either reaping with the scythe held low with both hands (as in the frescoes of Pritz and Roda de Isábena, on the facade of Arteta and on a capital of Santa María de Nieva) or in mid-swing with the scythe raised (as in the relief on the cathedral of Amiens) or sharpening a blade (as in Notre Dame in Paris) or even resting the scythe on one shoulder (Vienna and Fulda calendars), a posture that recalls the older personifications; in the Gerona Tapestry this iconography is given to the symbolic figure of Summer.

In Iberian calendars, reaping takes place in June (facade of Ripoll and the cloister of Tarragona), or July (San Isidoro de León, the facade of Beleña, the frescoes of Pritz, the frontal of Arteta, the cloisters of Pamplona and Nieva, the *Breviari d'amor*); however, in the Gerona Tapestry, the scene – which has virtually

Pamplona Cathedral

disappeared – belongs to August. Unlike hay, wheat is always cut with a sickle, usually one with a toothed blade, to avoid losing the grain from the ripe ears. This type of sickle is very common in the Spanish cycles and is shown as early as the tenth century in the *Beatos*. It can even be seen that the stalks are cut halfway down, so that the rest of the straw can be used for feeding livestock, for roofing or for kindling in winter.

Although reaping is always represented in the medieval cycles of the months, there were important developments in Castille at the end of the

Santa María de Nieva

twelfth century, when the theme was enriched by new motifs which, as M. A. Castiñeiras has pointed out, refer directly to the fierce heat of the plateau: the use of large straw hats for protection from the sun (illustrations for July and August in the *Breviari d'amor*), or the presence of earthenware pitchers for water, alluding to the thirst of the workers. Thus, in the reaping scene on a relief of the cloister of Tarragona, one of the reapers fills a cup from a pitcher and prepares to drink; in scenes of threshing the wheat on the threshing-floor various containers can be seen in the background; there is even a water jug hanging in a corner in

147

148

Beleña de Sorbe

the reaping scene on the facade of Beleña de Sorbe. According to Castiñeiras, the motif of summer thirst goes back to antiquity; it is represented in the August scene in the *Calendar of Philocalus* of 354. Allusions to the heat and sweat of field work can be linked, too, with a long literary tradition, as in the *Libro de Alexandre*:

> The month of July follows, reapers gathering the wheat,
> the sweat pours from their faces.
> Behind the animals follow the biting flies.

Once the wheat had been reaped, it was tied into sheaves and taken to the threshing-floor, as is shown in a relief on the facade of Santa María de Ripoll, in which a peasant, with the help of a woman, loads a sheaf on his shoulders; the same scene occurs, together with reaping, on a relief in the cloister of Tarragona. On the threshing-floor, two or three weeks after reaping, the grain is separated from the ears, a task appears in calendars for the month of August. PREPARING FOR THRESHING

In the early days the workers threshed with a flail, a tool that has its origin in the ancient Roman *perticae*; it is made up of two pieces of wood, the handle and the swingle, which is used to strike the wheat, and these are loosely held together by leather straps or metal rings, studied THRESHING WITH A FLAIL

Tarragona Cathedral

149

Roda de Isábena Cathedral   Breviari d'amor

and classified by Caro Baroja. This technique, the only one in use in France, was also common in Spain, as is shown in the medieval depictions in the Pantheon of San Isidoro de León, at Roda de Isábena and in the cloisters of Tarragona and Santa María de Nieva, as well as in the illustrations of the *Breviari d'amor*. The flail which was used until recently in the province of León is very similar to one depicted in the frescoes of the Pantheon of San Isidoro.

THE THRESHER The other system – the thresher – appears in calendars from the Iberian peninsula and represents an ancient agricultural tradition, cited by the Romans as native to Hispania. The thresher is a sledge consisting of three or four wooden planks slightly curved at the front. Pieces of flint or iron were inserted into the wood and the sledge was pulled by a team of oxen while the peasant sat on it; as it passed over the wheat, the straw and stalks would be crushed. Among the most ancient depictions is that on the facade of Beleña de Sorbe, from the end of the twelfth century, which shows in detail the thresher and the stalks below. It also appears on the facade of Arteta and on one of the bosses of the cloister of Pamplona, where there is a large stone on the thresher, as recommended in a text from the eighteenth century, quoted by Caro Baroja:

> If the man on the thresher considers that he needs more weight, he places large stones on top of it.

A similar method, but without the thresher, was used in Italy, according to the reliefs by Benedetto Antelami on Parma baptistery reliefs from the facade, of Ferrara cathedral: the task was carried out by oxen or horses trampling on the wheat laid out on the floor. This leaves the straw very short, so that it can be used for feeding livestock during the summer, as was the custom in Mediterranean countries.

3. Autumn

If summer is associated with scenes of reaping, the autumn is associated with the grape harvest, as in the Gerona Tapestry. In medieval calendars the vintage occupies the months of September and October, and there are plenty of examples showing the work beginning in August with the preparation of the barrels, as recommended by Piero de Crescenzi, the *Libro de Alexandre* and the *Libro de buen amor*. The theme is frequent in the Italian cycles of the twelfth and thirteenth centuries (the cathedral of Ferrara, Santa Maria della Pieve at Arezzo in Tuscany), a wooden mallet is commonly used for attaching or adjusting the barrel hoops, often supplemented with another, so that the barrel itself is not struck directly (Parma bapstistery, the Fontana Maggiore in Perugia and the facade of San Zeno in Verona). This iconography of the cooper, unknown in France, is also recorded in the north-eastern part of the Iberian peninsula, with an early example, earlier than those recorded from Italy, on the facade of Santa María de Ripoll, and other later ones like the September on the facade of Arteta – where, oddly, the vinatage itself is not shown. The interest of the Ripoll relief, apart from its date,

Parma Baptistery

lies in the action of the two figures: one readies himself to adjust the hoops with a hammer, while the other, who stands on a stool, carries a long stick for cleaning or tarring the barrel.

The grape harvest takes place at about the feast of St Michael (29 September) and is noted as a task of that month in the *Libro de Alexandre*:

> he harvested the vines
> with pruning knives.

This is also repeated in the *Libro de buen amor*:

> he begins to harvest
> grapes from the arbours.

In October, meanwhile:

> the third labourer
> tramples out the good
> wine,
> he fills all the casks like a
> good cellerman.

In depictions of the twelfth and thirteenth centuries, a single figure is preferred for representing the grape harvest, despite the fact that, as with reaping, it involved teamwork in which the whole family participated. It is possible that the preference is explained as a survival of the

155

ancient personifications, as in the *Fulda Calendar*, where September is a static figure in a frontal position below a trellis. In the Pantheon of San Isidoro de León, we can already see the tendency towards narrative action, where the labourer carefully cuts the bunches with one hand and places them in the basket that he holds in the other; this is also shown in a relief at Ripoll, where, exceptionally, a woman is assisting in the

San Isidoro de León, Panteón Real   Beleña de Sorbe

task. On the facade of Beleña de Sorbe is another variation: the labourer wields an enormous knife, while he holds the vine with the other hand, and the container, a large pannier made of esparto or wicker, rests on the ground. This is very close to the Italian examples in Parma and Ferrara. In the illustration of the *Breviari d'amor*, a billhook is used, on one side is a small, easily carried basket with a handle, which, when full, will be emptied into the wooden barrel depicted in the right-hand corner, which would be used to transport the grapes to the press.

The anecdotal and narrative feeling that characterizes the cycle of the months in the cloister of Tarragona is evident in the detail of the vines grown on supports, and in the animated gestures of the two people who work beneath the trellises. It is early, dated about 1200, but it already

prefigures the cheerful scenes of the grape harvest in the calendars of the fifteenth century.

This is also true of the depictions of treading the grapes, a subject that was very widespread in the fifteenth century and rare in the calendars of the twelfth and thirteenth centuries in Spanish calendars, although the

Breviari d'amor

scene was common enough at that time in France. Some of the French examples have individual touches, such as the September of the frescoes at Pritz, where the peasant cuts the clusters from the vine with one hand and tastes the fruit with the other, all the while treading the grapes in a large wooden vat.

In general, between the twelfth and fourteenth centuries, this scene is replaced by that of the transfer of the fermented wine from a wineskin to barrels or casks, depicted in detail: we can easily distinguish the wooden staves held together by hoops and vats carefully positioned on wooden feet so as to keep the wine off the ground. Among these cellar scenes, one of the most complete is the depiction of October in a relief in the cloister of Tarragona: the wine is drawn from the vat on the left, taken in a wineskin

and funnelled into the barrel on the right, whereas on a relief of the Fontana Maggiore in Perugia he uses a small cask. A simpler version, reduced to a single person, is found on the facade of Beleña de Sorbe, on a boss in the cloister in Pamplona, and on a capital of Santa María la Real in Nieva. In Spanish calendars, there are no references to wine tasting, but this is included in some French examples (Brinay), and also Italian ones (the mosaic of San Prospero in Reggio Emilia or that of Parma), or to later tasks such as topping off the casks as the wine diminishes in volume (due to the effects of fermentation, evaporation and the absorption of the wine into the wood of the barrels), a job that the *Libro de buen amor* allots to January:

Pamplona Cathedral

...he made them close the barrels, and fill them with funnels,
protecting them with plaster, since they carry unfinished wine.

THE AUTUMN PLOUGHING

The next task that occupies the peasant is the work of ploughing the land and sowing the winter seed for the next year, thus marking the cyclical continuity of the agricultural calendar. This work was carried out between St Martin's day – 11 November – and Christmas, as is reported in an Ordinance of the Courts of Valladolid of the year 1351, when it is stated that the following payments should be made:

And from St Martin's day until Christmas day, since they are the shortest days, to every pair of mules with a man for sowing or ploughing, three maravedis and a half per day; and to each pair of oxen with a man, two and a half maravedis per day; and to each pair of donkeys with a man, two maravedis.

However, in illustrated calendars, even though it sometimes occurs in November (Beleña de Sorbe, the cloister of Tarragona), the scene is more

Tarragona Cathedral

frequently given to October (facade of Arteta, the cloisters of Pamplona and Nieva). This lack of precision is reflected in the *Libro de buen amor*. Of October it says:

> take advantage of the weather for casting seed

and again in November:

> he commanded the wheat to be sown...

In general, the task was carried out before the rains arrived, using a team of oxen, the amount that one man could plough in one day with a pair of oxen was about an acre.

The October ploughing was shown in the cycles of antiquity, and it is very frequent in the calendars of the Mediterranean zone from the twelfth century, being particularly common in the region of Castille. As can be seen on a capital of the Nieva cloister, the peasant held the plough with one hand and in the other a goad for spurring on the oxen. The oxen were linked by a double yoke that rested on the back of their necks,with straw underneath to cushion them from the jolting of the plough: in the eleventh century the yoke was placed on the horns of the oxen in an attempt to overcome this problem.

159

Breviari d'amor

Sowing took place at the same time as or immediately after ploughing. As M. A. Castiñeiras has point-ed out, one of the unusual features of Spanish calendars is the conjunction of ploughing and sow-ing in the same scene; examples of this are the cycles of Beleña de Sorbe, the cloisters of Tarragona and Pamplona, and the facade of Arteta. With the excep-tion of the boss of the Pamplona cloister, where two people are involved – one controls the plough while the other casts the seeds – others show the labourer carrying out both tasks simultaneously, which justifies the use of the apron, a piece of cloth slung round the neck and held by the bent left arm, containing the seeds that are to be sown. The Castilian plough has a curved beam and is especially suit-ed to Mediterranean soils – it breaks up the top layer of the soil only, in contrast to the heavy, wheeled ploughs used in the wetter areas of Europe. At Beleña de Sorbe the peasant is shown preparing to cast the seeds that he takes from a sack. At his side he has a tool for compacting the earth so as to protect the seeds from birds. The scene even depicts the oxen team with yoke pads to protect them from the chafing of the yoke.

Perugia, Fontana Maggiore

Outside the Iberian peninsula, ploughing and seeding are generally separate tasks, and this is how they appear in two of the reliefs on the Fontana Maggiore in Perugia, although the sower usually, with a wide sweep of the right arm, casts the seeds on to a ploughed field. In Italy this scene usually is found in November, whereas in France it is often moved forward to October, because early sowing allows the roots to penetrate the soil before the onset of the cold and so to resist the frost. In Spain, too, some later cycles (from the fifteenth century on) show only sowing, as in the illustration in the *Breviari d'amor.*

When the seeding was finished, the farm labours that the peasant had to do throughout the year came to an end, yet before the winter break there was still one job to be done: killing the pigs. This animal was an

SOWING

KILLING OF THE PIGS

important part of the family economy, and the subject is often shown in the twelfth- and thirteenth- century calendars for the months of November or December; for October or November, the scene of fattening the pigs on acorns is still frequently included. At the end of autumn, the farmer takes the herd to the forest and beats the branches of the oak trees with a pole so that the animals can gorge themselves on the acorns, as in an illustration of the *Breviari d'amor*. The frequency of this scene in Spanish calendars seems to be intended to show that acorn gathering was included in the peasants' rights to grazing in the forest; it is included in early examples such as that of the Pantheon of San Isidoro de León and the façade of Santa María de Ripoll. In medieval inventories

San Isidoro de León, Panteón Real

wild boars are distinguished from domestic pigs, although the type of pig shown usually looks like a wild boar, with bristles, a long snout, protruding ears and long tusks, as on the façade of Arteta.

The slaughter scenes are perhaps the most expressive of the entire calendar; they are very varied, and illustrate the ingenuity of the methods used to immobilize the animal. In France an axe is generally used, held with both hands and with the blade facing out, in order to stun the

164

166

animal, a detail that can be seen on the Pantheon of San Isidoro, the facade of Ripoll or the boss of the Pamplona cloister, while in other examples, such as the cloister of Tarragona, the facade of Arteta or the illustration in the *Breviari d'amor*, the axe is replaced with a mallet. The way of holding the animal also varies, so that the man, if he is alone, uses his legs to straddle the pig, as on the cloister of Tarragona and the capital of the cloister in Nieva; sometimes an assistant holds the pig by its hind legs, as in the *Breviari d'amor*. In Italian calendars the scene normally depicted is the cutting of the pig's throat or the pig hanging from its hind legs so as to catch the blood, as in the relief on the Fontana Maggiore in Perugia. This scene on the facade of Beleña de Sorbe, unusually given to January, shows a man with a large knife preparing to quarter the animal lying on a chopping block.

4. THE WINTER REST

I n reality, the term 'rest' or 'repose' applied to this period is only justified by the lack of agricultural labour, since it corresponds to the months in which the seeds planted in November germinate. The peasant busies himself with other jobs, such as gathering firewood, tending livestock, making cheeses and even, as Alonso de Herrera, in the sixteenth century, recommends:

it is good to see to household chores, such as making tools, sealing barrels and cleaning vessels and wine cellars.

The winter tasks, since they are not linked directly to a particular month, do not normally appear in calendars; the illustrations for December, January and February are somewhat unspecific in their iconography, but they have two themes in common: food and fire. This is reflected also in the description of the three winter months in Don Amor's tent, in the *Libro de buen amor*.

Very close to the entrance, to the right,
is a table, rich and well made;
before it a fire, which gives out a great heat;
the three people at table cast glances at one another.

The table laden with food illustrates the feast, a creation of medieval THE FEAST
calendars for which there are no precedents in the cycles of antiquity. In
the first examples, of the twelfth century, it consists of a single man, seated
at a well-prepared table, and the scene may belong to either December or
January. One of the most ancient – the December of the Pantheon of San

San Isidoro de León, Panteón Real

Isidoro de León – has certain details which indicate iconographic contamination, a frequent feature of images of the winter months. The figure is dressed in an elegant mantle or Greek cloak fastened on the shoulder by a brooch, and prepares to eat by blessing a large loaf of bread. This is a unique gesture, unknown in other schemes, and has been interpreted as an allusion to the Eucharist. The solemnity of the gesture contrasts with the informality of his stockinged feet, which he raises to the warmth of a fire. This is inspired by the personification of winter as an elderly man warming himself by a fire, usually the scene for February in medieval cycles. On the other hand, the characterization of the man, with a short beard and rich clothing, indicates that he is not a peasant, who would normally be young and beardless, as shown in the depictions of agricultural labours in the other months of the San Isidoro calendar. Here we have one of the first instances of the nobleman's feast, a theme that reaches its full development in the cycles of the fifteenth century. There are two different

Beleña de Sorbe

interpretations of the feasting scene in calendars between the twelfth and sixteenth centuries: in some it is a scene from peasant life, the parties and feasting that mark the end of agricultural labours. That is how the December on the facade of Beleña de Sorbe, a depiction from the twelfth century, must be interpreted: the man seated at the table is the same worker who prunes the vines in March, weeds in June, reaps in July, threshes in August, harvests grapes in September, decants the wine in October and sows seed in November. In other cases, the nobleman's feast as shown at San Isidoro is repeated and is given more ceremonial, marked by the use of a tablecloth, plates, goblets and utensils, or by a greater number of people at the table, as in the Pamplona cloister boss or the capital in the cloister of Santa María de Nieva. In these months we frequently see the fusion of a classical theme – the image of the god Janus as the personification of January – with the medieval feast creating a new model, Janus at table; he may appear alone (the frescoes of Pritz, the illustration of the *Breviari*

The other major subject of illustrations of winter is obviously the cold. Already in the *Vienna Calendar* of the year 830, January appears as a young man bending over a fire to warm his hands; according to W. Endrei this iconography would be the result of medieval artists reinterpreting an illustration from calendars of antiquity of a man offering incense before sacrificial fires and converting it into an image for winter. The young January of the *Vienna Calendar* is replaced by the figure of an old man, shivering from the cold and wrapped in a thick cape and hood, following Hesiod's description of winter; this subject is

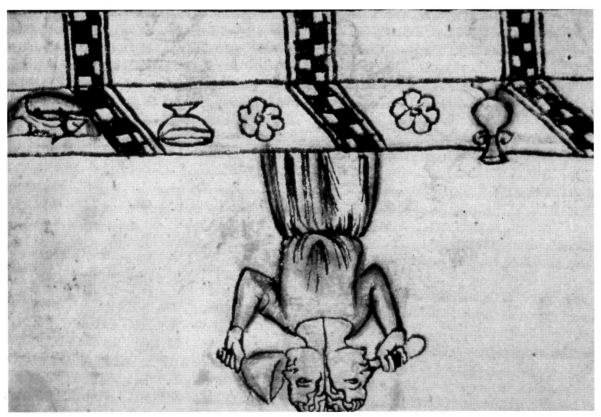

Breviari d'amor

d'amor) or attended by servants who bring food and drink, as on a relief in the cathedral of Amiens or the relief of the cloister of Tarragona. For the origin of this subject, which became widespread from the twelfth century, some have pointed to Italian calendars, where a rustic Janus is depicted in the kitchen watching a kettle hanging over the fire, as in Borgo San Donni-no, or drinking, with a large jug in his hand, as in San Giorgio at Ferrara, an image that may be also linked with the zodiac sign of Aquarius.

established in the Middle Ages as the usual illustration for February, the coldest and wettest month of the year. From the twelfth century on, new details begin to be added, following the narrative tendency of medieval calendars. Even in the earliest depictions we have the man raising an unshod foot in front of a fire, as in the *Martyrology of Wandalbert;* in the Pantheon of San Isidoro, he holds both hands and feet to the fire; frequently he is holding the boot that he has just taken off, as in the facade of Arteta, the frescoes of Pritz or the cloister of Pamplona. Often there is a kettle or cauldron hanging over the fire, a reminder of the January 'kitchen scenes'; sometimes a second person is attending to the

Santa María de Nieva

fire, as in the cloister of Tarragona or on a capital in the cloister of Nieva. The most unusual of all is the depiction of February at Beleña de Sorbe, where a peasant exposes his genitals over a fire. This seems to be linked to a reference in the *Codex Calixtinus* where, criticizing the customs of Vizcaya and Alava, it is pointed out that:

> both men and women in Navarra expose their shame
> as they warm themselves.

This might explain the presence of this subject on Romanesque capitals and corbels. It also appears in the illustration dedicated to the month of February in the *Très Riches Heures du Duc de Berry*, where the unconcerned attitude of the peasant couple contrasts with that of the woman in the foreground, who timidly lifts the edge of her skirt so as to warm her feet.

174

5. The Survival of the Agricultural Calendar in the Fifteenth Century

In the fifteenth century the illustrated calendar, which had fallen into disuse at the end of the thirteenth century, was given a new lease of life in the Books of Hours and missals of the well-to-do. This new context – quite different from that of the calendars in religious buildings which could be seen by everyone, including the peasants – brought about changes in the subject-matter of the cycles. Towards the end of the fourteenth century the aristocracy had adopted a more courtly lifestyle, and their interests and activities were reflected in the works that they commissioned, including many illuminated manuscripts. Thus the amusements of the nobility came to be substituted for the traditional images of the labours of the peasant in calendars. Nevertheless, since the countryside was the setting for their games and pastimes, agricultural tasks still appear in these 'calendars of the nobility', but the rural life is now idealized. The change in style is evident. The calendar scenes show the new interest in landscape which was a feature of the period. This appreciation of landscape – in the *Grandes Heures du Duc de Berry,*

exceptionally, it even becomes the sole subject of some scenes – gives rise to experiments with new types of composition, such as the snow-covered field which apppears in the illustration for February in the *Très Riches Heures*; new activities can now be depicted, such as the man felling a tree and another carrying a bundle of firewood, both in the same miniature. In these extensive outdoor scenes, farm tasks are mixed with scenes of carefree courtly life. The contrast in the social levels illustrated becomes a pretext for showing the good relationships of the landowners with the workers: they visit the peasants as they toil, are welcomed by them and carry on friendly conversations with them. They even participate in the peasants' tasks, as do the ladies of the October scene in the Torre Aquila in Trento who are picking and eating grapes.

Most strikingly, the peasants now carry out their work in groups; they are shown in harmonious poses and look more like costumed nobles than real labourers; they appear to be enjoying themselves, not wearing themselves out in exhausting toil.This can be clearly seen in the illustrations for June and July in the *Très Riches Heures* and in the July,

Trento, Castello del Buonconsiglio

Trento, Castello del Buonconsiglio

179

August and October frescoes at Trento. As well as the usual subjects – pruning vines in March, haymaking in June, reaping in July, the vintage in September or October, and ploughing or sowing seed in November – there are now subjects which are less common in earlier cycles, such as the spring ploughing and sowing in March at Trento. Other new motifs that are more typical of the fifteenth century are now introduced: sheep-shearing, included in the July scene in the *Très Riches Heures*, cheese-making in the June scene at Trento, sifting wheat in a large sieve in the August of the *Missal of Archbishop Carrillo* and diverse operations connected with wine-making: treading the grapes in the *Bedford Hours* and in the *Missal of Archbishop Carrillo*, pressing the grapes and tasting the must in the October at Trento, where a winepress worked by two men is portrayed in extraordinary detail.

Trento, Castello del Buonconsiglio

II The Calendar of
the Nobility

The nobleman or knight has little part to play in the predominantly agricultural calendars of the twelfth and thirteenth centuries; only in the fifteenth century, in the calendars in illuminated manuscripts, will he have a more important role. Before this date his only certainly identifiable appearance is in the depiction of the month of May, which in all the calendars from the twelfth century on, has a man riding a horse and carrying a falcon on his wrist, a clear indication of his social position.

As feudalism develops throughout the thirteenth and fourteenth centuries into a more courtly society, the nobility become more conscious of belonging to an aristocracy with a completely different lifestyle from that of the peasant. This concept of priviledge is given expression by attributes such as the falcon on the wrist and rich and elegant dress. There is a tendency towards increasing extravagance, and a taste for pomp and ceremony, for transforming daily life into a beautiful artifice. As J. Huizinga points out, to live 'nobly' at the end of the Middle Ages

Trento, Castello del Buonconsiglio

came to be synonymous with leading a life of refined frivolity, enjoying all the pleasures of the senses: pastimes, outdoor games and sports, hunts, banquets, dances and parties...activities that require the participation of the group, and so can best be pursued at court. Of the three orders that Aldalberon of Laón enumerated at the beginning of the eleventh century, the soldier was transformed into a courtier and, having forgotten his military exploits, sought to disguise the realities of his life through fantasy, the ceremonial forms of palace life.

This new aesthetic of aristocratic life would transform the decoration of everything that made up its surroundings, beautifying palaces with paintings and tapestries, adorning personal objects, chests, coffers, mirrors or ivory combs, manuscripts...and even the calendars that were included at the beginning of Books of Hours. The themes of the agricultural cycle, which had formed the basis of earlier calendars, are maintained for the most part, but the lone peasant is now replaced by a

183

group scene: well-dressed and cheerful workers are scattered in a open landscape, and may even become a backdrop to the pursuits of the nobility in the foreground. It is rare for the diversions of the courtly life to be the only subject, as in the tournament, for February in the frescoes in the Torre Aquila in Trento – difficult to relate to the carnival season – or the astonishing image, also at Trento, of a frozen and desolate January landscape with knights and ladies in elegant, light and even low-cut costumes having a snowball fight in front of a castle, identified as the castle of Stenico, renovated by Bishop Georges of Liechtenstein, whose banners wave above the towers and who commissioned the frescoes of Trento.

1. From May the Warrior to May the Knight

In the scene for May in the Pantheon of San Isidoro de León, there is a man with his horse, which is saddled and ready to ride; he holds it by the reins, and has a shield in his other hand. He is obviously a warrior and his presence in the calendar among the agricultural labours has been justified as a survival of a custom dating back to ancient Greece, where military campaigns were initiated at the end of winter, when the cold weather and rains had passed. Again, it was common among the Romans to hold a troop review in spring in honour of Mars, the god of war – 'Campus Martius' – and so the month of March came to be dedicated to him. This tradition was carried on during the Middle Ages, but from 755, after the reform of Pépin the Short, the date of the review was moved to May in order to coincide with the beginning of hostilities.

Regarding the inclusion of the warrior in the cycle of the months, there is a reference in the *Libro de Alexandre*, although in this case it refers to April:

April emerged ready to go to war,
with the barley fields ready for reaping.

In illustrated calendars the knight on horseback is always found in May,
as in the MAGGIVS of San Isidoro de León, and various examples from
France (Brinay, Autun) and Italy: a well-armed warrior with helmet and
shield is depicted astride a horse (Ferrara cathedral) and even prepared
for combat, with his lance at the ready, at San Donnino in Fidenza and
at San Zeno in Verona.

Parma Baptistery

From the end of the twelfth century on, the subject undergoes a transformation: the knight abandons his weapons and acquires a typically aristocratic image, the nobleman who carries a falcon on his

Breviari d'amor

188

wrist as his attribute. In one of the first examples – the May of the facade of Beleña de Sorbe – the figure is not differentiated from those in the other scenes in his physical appearance or in his clothing, but he proudly displays the falcon on his gloved hand, an allusion to the practice of falconry, which was reserved to knights and noblemen. The same scene is repeated on a cloister boss at Pamplona cathedral, on the facade of Arteta and in an illustration of the *Breviari d'amor*, always as a personification of May, and it is similar to the figure on a relief in the cloister of Tarragona who, although he does not hold a falcon, expresses his nobility through the elegant gesture of his hand resting on the hindquarters of his horse.

In Pamplona the horseman has, as usual, a falcon, and also holds a flowering branch in his other hand, together with the reins. This motif is important because it suggests the iconographic contamination from the

Notre Dame de Pritz

usual image of April as the allegory of spring, with bunches of flowers in both hands. The subject is already perfectly defined at the beginning of the thirteenth century in the May of the frescoes of Pritz, where the horseman, without a falcon, holds a delicate flower stem in his right hand; the way he sits on the narrow saddle and his luxurious mantle lined with ermine confirm his state as a knight. On the other hand, if we compare this image with the representation of April in this and other calendars, we note that there is a clear difference: whereas April is depicted standing and facing the front, a reminder of its origin in the personifications of antiquity, May is always a horseman of elegant and courtly appearance, and prefigures the first appearance of the upper class in the agricultural calendars of the twelfth and thirteenth centuries,

189

which are based on the peasant life. The image would persist for the representation of May in numerous manuscripts during the fifteenth century, as in the *Bedford Hours.*

A unique case of iconographic interference is found on a capital of the cloister of Santa María la Real de Nieva, where both April and May, wearing doublet and hose in the international style of the day, ride horses and hold plants in their hands. The first, April, carries a flowering branch, while May – with a falcon on his hand and crowned with flowers – holds a small tree over his shoulder. This motif, which on one hand is connected with other depictions that allude to the rebirth of vegetation in April, can also be interpreted as a reference to maypole of popular folklore.

Santa María de Nieva

2. The Spring Outing

The association between spring and the image of the knight, which characterizes the iconography of May in the calendars of the twelfth and thirteenth centuries, is the forerunner of a group of fifteenth-century illustrations of the pastimes of knights and ladies during the months of April, May and June. Gathering flowers and fruit in the fields, dancing in a ring, picnicking or riding in the woods are some of their open-air amusements; these scenes emphasize social differences, for they contrast with the work of the peasants which appears in the background. The *Très Riches Heures du Duc de Berry* and the scenes of the months in the Torre Aquila in Trento both contain excellent examples.

193

Trento, Castello del Buonconsiglio

The enjoyment of nature seems to explain the taste for landscapes of green meadows and forests, bursting into flower and new leaf, exuberant vegetation that in French is called *verdure*, and in Spanish *floresta*. The colour of living green (the *vert gai*) dominates not only the countryside, but also the clothing and adornments of the people. At the end of the fourteenth century, the festival of the first of May was famously celebrated in the court of France: King Charles V gave his courtiers and friends gifts of green garments, known as *la livré de mai*. They are shown in the May scene of the *Très Riches Heures*: behind a knight dressed in blue with a rich gold necklace, who some identify as the duke himself, are three ladies in green gowns riding horses with green trappings on their harnesses. The ladies and all the others wear garlands round their necks, on their head-dresses or in their hair. The celebration of the first of May included a procession through the countryside carrying branches of blossom, in memory of the ancient Roman *floralia*, thus perpetuating the custom of wearing green on that day to symbolize the

Trento, Castello del Buonconsiglio

rebirth of nature. As well as referring to the May Day festival, the miniature in the *Très Riches Heures du Duc de Berry* illustrates the aristocratic pastime, the outing on horseback for the sole pleasure of riding. One of the texts of Christine de Pisan alludes to this:

…one day, to enjoy ourselves, we went riding.

In the paintings of the cycle of the months at Trento, May and June again have scenes of country outings, in this case on foot, of parties composed mostly of young couples. In June, they are walking in the woods and the vivid green of the dresses is striking. Some of them are wearing extravagant hats, and all have long, elegant gowns that trail on the ground. The ground itself is carpeted with minutely drawn plants, including lilies in bloom; it looks like one of the tapestries that were woven in the workshops of Arras at the end of the fifteenth century. The enjoyment of nature and the pleasures of conversation are accompanied

Trento, Castello del Buonconsiglio

by tunes from the group of musicians at the back – an idea that would be developed later in the so-called *'concert champêtre'.*

Somewhat more complex is the composition for May. The group begins to disperse, and isolated couples occupy the scene: in the background, two couples are seated at a table laden with food, elegantly covered with a tablecloth and utensils, by a fountain, a motif that suggests themes such as the "Garden of Love" or the "Fountain of Youth". Other couples are seated on the grass and flowers, and some of the young people have made garlands for their heads; wild roses abound, the flower so dear to lovers. Everything points to the fact that the spring outing has developed into a scene of courtship, located here in the most favourable month, as the *Libro de Alexandre* tells us:

> The month of May, a glorious time,
> when the birds create a wonderful sound,
> the fields are clothed in beautiful attire,
> and the unwed maiden sighs.

The Trento scene is thus centred on the theme of the amorous pursuit, with its gallant talk and tender gestures, always within the respectful limits of courtly love. In the centre foreground, a lady holds a crown of flowers, which she is about to place on the head of the knight who kneels before her. This marks the beginning of intimacy between the lovers since, in the formalized language of courtly love, the posture of the knight, with one knee on the ground, shows that he has just declared his love to the lady, and she has expressed her acceptance of it by placing on his head the crown of flowers she has made.

The giving of other objects, such as rings or jewels, also played an important role in courtship. In the illustration for April in the *Très Riches Heures* a lady receives the ring that a knight offers her. The presence of another couple seems to indicate that this is a betrothal scene, taking place before witnesses, and it has been suggested that the lady may be the granddaughter of the Duke de Berry, Bonne d'Armagnac, who was betrothed at that time to the future Duke of Orléans. In any case it should be pointed out that the event takes place in a spring meadow; two elegant ladies, slightly apart from the main group, are bending down to gather flowers.

196

198

3. THE HUNT

During the Middle Ages, hunting was the main recreation for kings and nobles. Alfonso X, in his *Partidas*, recounts the advantages of hunting:

> ...one of the most beneficial things that the ancients did is hunting, of any kind: it helps to lessen the burden of angry thoughts...it is healthy, since the exercise that is involved in it, if done in good measure, causes one to eat and sleep well, which is the best thing for the life of a man. And the pleasure that one receives from it is a great joy at having power over the birds of the air and the wild beasts and making them obey him and serve him.

200

Don Juan Manuel echoes this in his *Libro de los estados*:

> There is nothing that so befits a knight as being a hunter in the mountains…and I tell you that among the many good things to be had from the hunt are these: first, that a man learns to endure great labours, that he becomes healthy and eats better and knows the land and its ways and its passes, and learns to be more generous and more sincere…

Numerous extant medieval treatises on hunting bear witness to its popularity, describing animals and the different systems for catching them, explaining the use of the right tools, nets and every type of trap. Among the best known of these were the *Tractatus de arte venandi* of Frederick II of Sicily, the *Livre du Roi Modus*, the *Livre de chasse* of Gaston Phébus, Count of Foix, written in 1387, of which there are at least thirty-seven illuminated copies; it was later imitated in the *Master of Game* by Edward II, Duke of York. Among Spanish texts, in addition to the *Libro de la montería* of Alfonso XI, there was the *Libro de la caça* of Don Juan Manuel. There were also treatises on falconry, such as the *Libro de la caça de las aves* by the Chancellor Don Pedro López de Ayala, and the *Livro de falcaria* by Pero Menino, falconer to King Fernando I of Portugal. In all of them are miniatures which show us details of the methods and customs used in the Middle Ages.

Among the different types of hunt, falconry and hunting on horseback were practised by the nobility, and both are shown in fifteenth-century calendars. Originating in the East, falconry – hunting with birds of prey – was known but rarely practised by the Romans, which suggests that it was introduced to the Iberian peninsula through the Moorish kingdom of al-Andalus, where, at the end of the eighth century, according to the chronicles, al-Hakam I practised falconry and Abd al-Rahmam II hunted cranes with hawks in the Guadalquivir valley. It must have spread to the Christian kingdoms soon after, given that in the will of Alfonso II dated 812 some goshawk chicks in a forest are bequeathed by the monarch to the cathedral of Oviedo. Falconry was inevitably an indication of high rank, a sport confined to kings and nobles, due to the high cost of obtaining, raising and training the birds. The trained hawks were highly prized; an idea of their value is given in a ballad describing the departure of El Cid into exile:

201

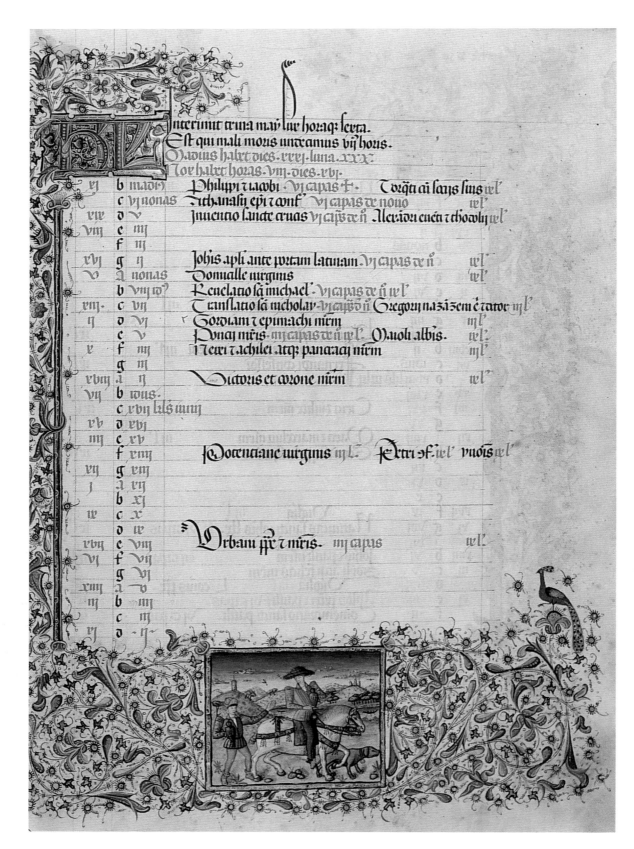

Missal of Archbishop Alonso Carrillo de Acuña

He leaves behind spaniels and greyhounds,
he only takes his falcons, and their chicks.

In addition to falcons, among which the most prized were the *nebli*, a variety raised in the region of Niebla, the gerfalcon and the lanner were used for stooping from a height, and the goshawk and the sparrowhawk for low-flying prey.

On calendars, falconry was always given to August and September. In the *Très Riches Heures* of the Duke of Berry the moment of setting off is depicted, when falconers and grooms were followed by the nobles on horseback, each of whom carried on his fist, protected by a thick glove, a falcon with its head covered by a leather hood which was removed at the moment of releasing it after the prey. In the miniature, however, the scene has something of the appearance of an amorous game: the ladies are riding pillion and everyone is wearing elegant gowns and elaborate hats, but the subject is clearly identified by the falcons that they hold and the presence of the falconer who leads on foot. The same elements, the falcon and the falconer, allow us to identify as a hawking scene the lone knight in the miniature for May in the *Missal of Archbishop Carrillo*.

Trento, Castello del Buonconsiglio

In the cycle of the months at Trento there are various references to falconry. In July, two servants carry falcons perched on poles; on the left, the method of attaching the birds can be clearly seen: leather thongs (jesses) are tied to the bird's legs and a leash is tied to the perch, allowing the bird to fly while still on the leash. The two people in the foreground may be tying these leashes, although the half-kneeling position of the knight recalls the rituals of courtship.

The scene that appears in the fresco for August, should, I think, be interpreted as the training of the birds: in an

203

enclosed garden planted with fruit trees, two ladies hold falcons while a man motions to a falcon perched on a rock, showing it something that is probably a rodent or a lure. I don't know of any other depiction of this theme, although it is described in detail in treatises on hunting, since the care and training of falcons was a specialized task entrusted to a falconer, a highly responsible post in medieval courts. A passage of the *Libro de la caça de las aves* of the Chancellor Don Pedro López de Ayala could be related to this scene:

> On the day that your falcon does not need to fly, in the morning put him on a rock in the meadow, in a retired place, tied well by his leash, and there he will sit and think to himself; and make sure that the place where you put him is enclosed, and not an open field, otherwise he will see the birds flying above and will not rest. And stay near him with a lure, so that if you see that he does not want to rest, you can fly him. This way of placing the falcon in the meadow is not used by the hunters of Castille, but the Brabante falconer would not give it up for anything in the world, because he says that his falcon needs to think to himself, and take pleasure in it, and that it is better for him there than on his perch.

204

205

Trento, Castello del Buonconsiglio

Regarding the handling of falcons by ladies, which is also seen in other hunting scenes, López de Ayala describes *neblí* falcons that:

> in France are named falcons of the *dames*, which means ladies' falcons; and they are very beautiful, docile to train, and of good disposition…and they make good heron hunters. In Castille the falconers and hunters call them 'maidens'.

Lastly, in September the hunt reaches its height: in the foreground a knight and two ladies have released a falcon that swoops upon the prey and, in the centre of the scene, two knights illustrate two consecutive moments: the one on the left holds a falcon on his hand, while the one on the right has already released his bird after a flock of partridges put up by the dogs. This horseman has a small bag hanging from his belt, which López de Ayala describes as among the necessary equipment that the hunter must carry for himself:

> He must also bring his small cloth bag, made so that it hangs at his side, in which he can put the ducks or other prey that the falcon takes, hiding them so that the falcon cannot see them, and in which he can carry food for the falcon, rodents, an extra hood and bells, in case he wants to leash or unleash his falcon.

HUNTING When hunting on horseback, dogs were frequently used: greyhounds were much prized, but also mastiffs, great danes, spaniels and other types of hounds. Their role was to pick up the scent and pursue the prey until the hunter arrived to finish it off, usually with a javelin. Among the coveted animals were bears, wild boars, stags, fallow deer and roe deer, and even the mountain goat of the Pyrenees for the kings of Aragon. In medieval texts the designation of game applies to everything that is hunted; sometimes there is a distinction between 'black' game (bear and wild boar) and 'red' game (deer and stags).

As with falconry, the departure for the hunt has the aspect of a solemn procession in fifteenth-century depictions: the knights, accompanied by their ladies, are followed by the hunters – also on horseback – and behind them the servants on foot, crossbowmen, archers, boys to look

after the hounds...Even though it was a frequent theme in paintings, miniatures and tapestries, it does not appear in calendars, which focus on the hunt and the kill. In the month of November in the Trento cycle, a bear hunt is shown – according to the *Livre de chasse* by Gaston Phébus, the hunting season began in May and lasted until the rut in December. He also points out that bears must be tracked with bloodhounds:

> in order to hunt them and capture them quickly you need mastiffs crossed with bloodhounds

since the bear, on being attacked,

> bites them, smothers them and wounds them seriously, and if I had good, handsome greyhounds, I would have much sorrow in losing them.

Moreover,

> you must have archers or crossbowmen, or both, and good, solid javelins. Those on horseback must strike from a distance with lances or darts, and not come close in with sword in hand as one does with a boar, since it would grab them by the neck and embrace them mercilessly.

Trento, Castello del Buonconsiglio

207

In the Trento scene, some of these practices are shown: a bear, perhaps a mother with its two cubs, is pursued by dogs that seem to be mastiffs – certainly not greyhounds – while the servants, having already surrounded the prey, watch from a distance, on foot and armed with javelins. One holds on to a pack of dogs, and another, on the opposite side, prepares to sound the horn, probably the signal for slipping the hounds which will close off the bear's escape route. Farther away, two knights, also carrying javelins, wait for the opportunity to capture the bear and another group, who have dismounted, are talking around a fire at the meeting-point.

The illustration of the *Très Riches Heures* for December shows a boar hunt and, given that in calendars this month is normally identified with killing

Les Très Riches Heures du Duc de Berry

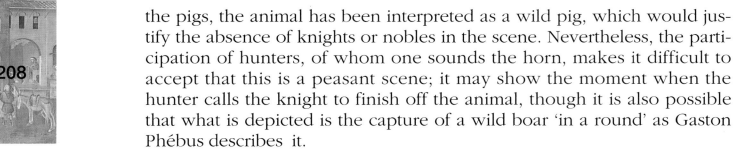

the pigs, the animal has been interpreted as a wild pig, which would justify the absence of knights or nobles in the scene. Nevertheless, the participation of hunters, of whom one sounds the horn, makes it difficult to accept that this is a peasant scene; it may show the moment when the hunter calls the knight to finish off the animal, though it is also possible that what is depicted is the capture of a wild boar 'in a round' as Gaston Phébus describes it.

4. THE BANQUET

Of all the miniatures of the *Très Riches Heures* for the Duke de Berry, the best known is the one for the month of January, showing the New Year's banquet. It has been the subject of intense study, and is considered to be a faithful record of a real event: the celebration of the New Year, when the duke would give and receive gifts. Seated at the table he presides over the ceremony dressed in a luxurious blue gown embroidered in gold and lined with fur; it seems to be a portrait of the Duc de Berry himself, who was about seventy when the painting was done. The prelate on his right is thought to be his protégé, the Bishop of Luçon, or perhaps Martin Gouge, Bishop of Chartres, who, like the duke, was a great collector of manuscripts. Moreover, among those that the chamberlain ushers in with the words '*aproche, aproche*', P. Durrieu claimed, years ago, to recognize the Limbourg brothers, miniaturists in the Duke's service, and painters of much of the *Très Riches Heures*. The scene could have taken place in the great hall of the palace of Bourges. It is known that in 1385 a tapestry depicting a battle scene was made for that hall, and it could well be the one shown here hanging at the back of the room illustrating a scene from the Trojan War. Other details also display a good knowledge of the court of Berry: the decoration on the canopy showing the duke's coat of arms accompanied by the emblems of a bear and a swan, interpreted as an allusion to Ursine (from the French words for bear and swan: *ours* and *cigne*), the name of a lady beloved by the duke. The same animals appear at either end of the nef or ship, the duke's '*salière du Pavillon*' which is conspicuously placed on the table, and is mentioned in the duke's inventories. Beside it, two puppies are licking a plate clean, calling to mind the little 'tou-tous' that the Duke liked to keep near him.

Going beyond the specific occasion, the miniature illustrates the con-

spicuous display of power that was the purpose of the banquet in the courtly circles of the late Middle Ages. The banquet takes place at several tables, and sometimes in several rooms, with the high table, occupied by the lord, by himself or with the guest of honour if he was of sufficient rank, given importance by being placed on a platform or dais. The remaining diners are seated at other tables, their rank indicated by their proximity to the lord's table. Only when the meal was finished, and when invited to do so, could they come forward to greet the host, who remained seated at his table; this is the moment that is shown in the miniature of the *Très Riches Heures*, when the chamberlain addresses the guests who are standing at the side of the Duke's table, waiting to express their greetings and good wishes for the New Year.

The tables consisted of boards resting on trestles, hidden by rich tablecloths, so that once the banquet was finished they could be quickly cleared away and the hall could be used for dances or

Les Très Riches Heures du Duc de Berry

211

shows. On the table there would be a salt-cellar and bread, while the utensils and plates were generally shared between two; books of etiquette always insist that hands and knife must be clean. This is what Pedro Alfonso advises in his *Disciplina clericalis*:

> When you have washed your hands before eating, touch nothing other than the food...Wash your hands after eating because it is polite and healthy; many cause irritation in their eyes, because they rub them after eating with unwashed hands...

Les Très Riches Heures du Duc de Berry

At the lord's table was the ship, as it appears in the Duc de Berry's banquet scene; this was a valuable piece, either in gold or silver, engraved and often adorned with enamels or precious stones. It was used to keep the utensils, cup, napkin and salt used by the master of the house. Great lords would possess many of these; in the inventories of the Duke of Anjou, for example, thirty-one are mentioned. The comfit box, too, would be placed on the table, a box with compartments for each of the spices that were taken after the meal, and these boxes are also listed in the inventories of the era. The plate was arranged on shelves or on a 'sideboard' to display them (as shown on the left side of the miniature), since possessing a rich set of gold tableware with numerous pieces was a clear sign of wealth, and the ostentatious display of wealth was the ulterior aim of the banquet.

The same applied to the food: the variety and number of the dishes demonstrated the prodigality, wealth and generosity of the lord. Thus what was known as '*service à la francais*' could include five courses per meal, each made up of several dishes, and each guest might eat one or two dishes at each course; this made it possible to serve, at the same course, dishes that were of better quality for the lord and his guests of honour, and other, less refined dishes for the rest of the diners. After an appetizer or opening dish – sweet *garnacha* wine accompanied by pastries and fruit, usually baked apples, cherries or plums – they moved on to vegetables, fish and roast meats, rounding the meal off with a variety of savouries and, as a finishing touch, the dessert, consisting of different types of preserves, pastries and dried fruit. Afterwards, at the most sumptuous feasts, hippocras was offered; a type of mulled wine, accompanied by cookies and light pastries. In the thirteenth century, Arnaldo de Vilanova gives this recipe for making the drink in his *Liber de vinis*:

> Take of cubeb [peppery Javanese spice berries], cloves, nutmeg and raisins, one ounce each; wrap it all in a piece of cloth and boil it in three pounds of good wine until they are reduced to two. Add sugar.

213

In addition to service '*à la francais*', there were other ways of serving a meal, varying in the order and composition of the dishes; in Catalonia in the fourteenth century the grilled meats were served before the vegetables, and in England all the courses included roasted meats.

The complexity of the banquet ceremony would require a large number of servants, both in the kitchen for the preparation of the dishes and in the hall for distributing the food among the guests. Strict rules of etiquette were followed and they are described in treatises on cooking and manuals of manners of the era, many of which have been preserved. These texts give details which do not appear in the illustrations. The service for the prince's or lord's table involved three different officials. The yeoman of the pantry, whose job it was to cut the bread and bring the salt, also placed the ship on the table. The cup-bearer was in charge of pouring the wine; in the miniature of the Duc de Berry's banquet he appears on the left, by the sideboard with the table settings, carrying out a ceremony that is described at about the same date by Olivier de la Marche, in the *Estat de la maison du duc Charles de Bourgogne*:

> When the lord arrives at the banquet hall and takes his seat, the steward calls the cup-bearer, who leaves the table and goes to the sideboard. There he finds the receptacles that the butler or yeoman of the cellar has prepared; he takes them, rinses them with water and returns them. Once this has been done, the cup-bearer takes a cup and looks at the lord, and he must do it so attentively that the lord need only nod in order to ask for more wine. Once the nod has been given, the cup-bearer takes the cup in his hand, and a bowl, and raises the cup up so that his breath does not reach it. The marshal of the hall lets him pass and when the butler sees him coming, he fills a ewer with fresh water, and rinses the cup that the cup-bearer brings, both inside and out. He then takes a bowl in his left hand and a jug in the right, and pours wine first into the bowl that he himself holds, and then into the cup that the cup-bearer holds. He then takes the ewer and pours water into the bowl, and then adjusts the wine that is in the cup, according to his expertise and what he knows of the tastes of the lord and his disposition. [This is the moment that appears in the miniature.] Once the wine has been decanted, the cup-bearer pours wine from the cup into the bowl that he is holding and covers the cup, holding the lid of the cup between the two little

214

fingers of the hand with which he holds the bowl, until he has covered the cup and given what he poured into the bowl to the butler, who has to taste it in front of him. After that, the cup-bearer takes the cup to the lord and uncovers it, pours wine into the bowl, covers the cup again and tastes the wine. When the lord puts forth his hand, the cup-bearer gives him the uncovered cup, and holds the bowl beneath the cup [to catch any drips] until the lord has finished drinking.

The insistence on the necessity of covering the cup and particularly on the elaborate ceremony of tasting the wine is explained by the frequency of poisoning in the Middle Ages. Unicorn's horn was widely used as a precautionary measure, for it would turn black in the presence of poison or any other noxious substance. In the text quoted earlier, Olivier de la Marche points out:

the lord's jug should be distinguished by the piece of unicorn horn hanging from a cord.

Les Très Riches Heures du Duc de Berry

It is possible that unicorn horn is what is hanging on the cup-bearer's belt with his purse in the miniature of the *Très Riches Heures*; it seems to be identical to one that the meat-carver has in the same scene, and in his case it would be used for testing the condition of the meat. A high price was paid for these horns; more reasonable, though of equally doubtful value, is the advice of Ruperto da Nola, cook to the king of Naples, in his *Libro de cozina*, from the end of the fifteenth century:

215

> But really, and in truth, great lords should not drink from any but glass goblets. Better still, from the very fine glass known as *selicornio*, because in this glass it is impossible to give poison since the good glass will not hold it without breaking. And for this reason, great lords must drink first in glass goblets, and not in ones made from gold or silver.

Finally, the third official serving at the lord's table was the carver, who was in charge of cutting the meat for the lord and serving him, and had the right to eat any leftover pieces from the meat he had prepared for the lord. The food, too, was frequently tested for poison, using unicorn horn and also small knives called 'serpents' tongues'. In the miniature of the Duc de Berry, the carver is carrying out his function, facing the duke, wearing a luxurious silk tunic; he is also wearing spurs, indicating that he is a knight, for the office of carver was one of the highest, restricted to the noble youths who were educated at court.

The illustration of the New Year's banquet in the *Très Riches Heures* is unique – it uses the traditional January image as a pretext for including in a religious manuscript, a Book of Hours, a scene promoting the duke and his lineage. Nevertheless, some elements – the table laden with food, the fire in the hearth - help to link this painting with the long tradition of illustrations of the winter feast in medieval calendars. As early as the Pantheon of San Isidoro de León, the image for December had been given a new, more aristocratic iconography, instead of the simple peasant's meal which had appeared in the agricultural cycle of the calendars of the twelfth and thirteenth centuries. This alternative iconography was then repeated in a boss in the cloister at Pamplona, on a capital at Santa María la Real in Nieva and in various other places. Thus in some of the cycles from the twelfth to the fourteenth centuries the lord's banquet for December or January (along with the depiction of a knight with a falcon in May) is an early indication of the change which would take place in calendars from the late fourteenth century on, when they came to be used to illustrate aristocratic pursuits – perhaps, as Huizinga suggests, because the nobility aspired to the life beautiful, so reinforcing the cohesion of the courtly class.

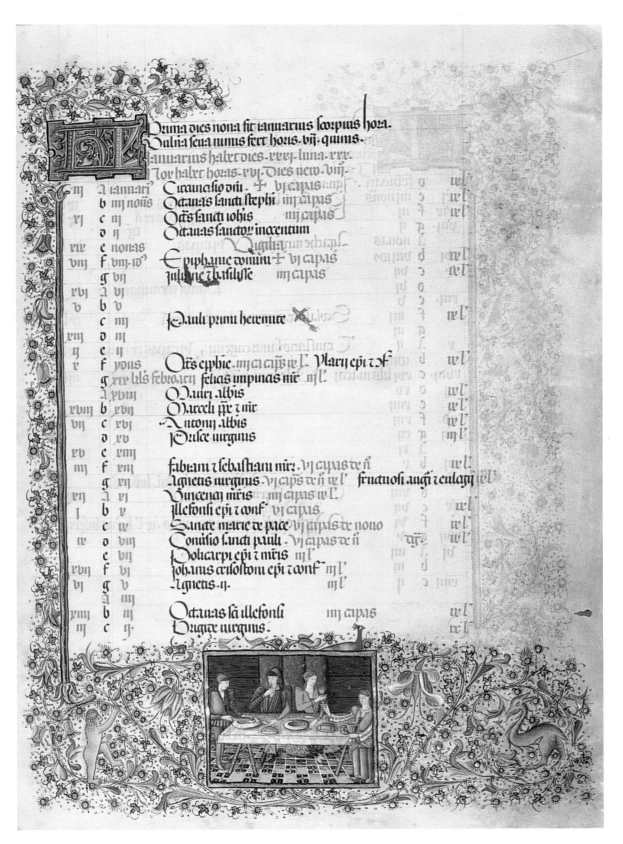

Missal of Archbishop Alonso Carrillo de Acuña

The January banquet in the calendars of the fifteenth century generally includes only one or two people, and so the ceremonial that accompanies the scene is necessarily limited. This is evident, for example, in the vignette for January in the *Missal of Archbishop Carrillo*: a couple, noble, as can be seen from their clothing, sits at a table without plates or silver, while a young maid serves wine (directly from the jug to the cup without any preliminary tasting) and a page carves the meat, which the couple will have to eat with their hands, with bread, the only other food that appears on the table. In some calendars of the fifteenth century yet another aspect of the subject is recorded: the meal of the new social class, the well-to-do merchants, for whom the aristocratic banquet served as a model. Although they dined without the elaborate ceremony of the nobles, the table was well supplied and the meal took place in a comfortable room with a generous fire, the iconographic focus of the theme. However, only the men participated, served by the master's wife, who rarely appears seated at the table. This formula, quite common in Flemish miniatures, became more widespread at the end of the century through the popularity of the *Grant Kalendrier des bergiers*.

According to Adalberon de León and Gerard of Cambray, prayer was the function assigned to clerics by society. In the Middle Ages several new religious Orders were founded, each with its own Rule reflecting the reforms they wanted to bring about: greater dedication to the divine offices, to intellectual pursuits in the scriptoria, to manual labour, to preaching, to asceticism and penance ... But the liturgy, which regulated the religious life of monks and clerics, imposed the observances of the church year on everyone.

The liturgical calendar corresponds to an annual cycle that runs from the first Sunday in Advent to the last Sunday after Pentecost, evoking the mysteries of the life of Christ: his birth, epiphanies, teaching, Passion, death, resurrection and ascension, and also the coming of the Holy Ghost to the apostles. The first part of the cycle to be established, the *Pascua Crucifixionis* and the *Pascua Resurrectionis,* was based on the

Passion of Christ and his death and resurrection. Later, between the second to the fourth centuries, a period of penitential preparation, Lent, was added to this nucleus, along with another period of fifty days after the Resurrection, known as Pentecost. Finally, in the fourth century, a second nucleus was formed around the birth of Christ, completing the evocation of his life. This consisted of Christmas, which also had its own period of preparation, Advent, and a period of prolongation, Epiphany, which included the feasts of the Magi, the baptism of Christ and the wedding at Cana.

In short, by the fourth century the two great liturgical cycles, Christmas and Easter, had already taken shape, and around them all the feasts universally celebrated by the Church. At first the liturgical year began on 25 March, coinciding with the spring equinox, the day on which, according to tradition, the world had been created, and also the date of the the Incarnation, the Annunciation to the Virgin of the birth of Christ. However, from the fourth century on, when the feast of Christmas had been introduced, the celebration of the Annunciation was transferred in many churches to the Advent period so as not to coincide with Lent. The liturgical year was then definitively established as beginning at the start of Advent, which obviously does not coincide with the twelve-month Julian calendar of the secular year. Liturgical cycles were important to the marking of the passage of time in the Middle Ages. The most important events of man's life – birth, marriage and death – were set in a religious context, and the passing of the days and months was marked by the celebrations of the religious feasts. Just as the tasks of the agricultural year were incorporated into the iconography first of the churches and cathedrals and then, in the fifteenth century, of Books of Hours and missals, integrating the peasant into the universal Church and its promise of redemption, so the religious festivals ensured the participation of lay people in the life of the Church.

From the very beginning of the Christian era, pagan feasts were absorbed into Christian ones; many references connecting the cycle of nature and Christian feast days still persist today in popular folklore, as has been pointed out by J. Caro Baroja. The Circumcision was made to coincide with the Saturnalia, the Roman celebration of the new year, the Major Rogation (25 April), with the rites of spring (the Robigalia), and the feast of John the Baptist with the summer solstice. In addition, the new

221

festivals established by the Church in honour of its saints were often linked to agricultural tasks or activities, and traces of these links are preserved in numerous sayings. The following examples are from the Iberian peninsula:

> *A cada puerco le llega su San Martin* (Every pig has his St Martin's day);
> *Por San Francisco siembra el trigo; la vieja que lo decia ya sembrado lo tenia* (On St Francis's day, sow the wheat; the old woman who said that had already done it);
> *Agua por San Juan, quita vino y no da pan* (Rain on St John's day takes away wine and gives no bread);
> *Por San Gil, nogueras a sacudir* (Shake the walnuts down on St Giles's day) or *Por San Urban, vendimia tu nogal* (On St Urban's day, harvest your walnuts);
> *Por San Vicente, alza la mano de simiente* (On St Vincent's day, raise your hand to sow);
> *Desde el dia de San Bernabé, se saca la paja por el pie* (After St Barnabas's day, pull up the hay);
> *Por San Lucas, bien saben las uvas* (On St Luke's day, the grapes taste good);
> *Hasta San Juan, todo vino es rabadan* (Until St John's day, all wine is fit to drink)
> ... and many others.

During the Middle Ages it became customary to combine liturgical ceremonies and offices with the church festivals in order to bring the faithful closer to the life of Christ by dramatizing the events of his infancy, Passion and resurrection.

Liturgical drama is recorded in western churches and monasteries from the ninth and tenth centuries on; the idea was to give vitality to the liturgy, first of all by interpolating brief phrases into a religious text, but soon this took the form of a dialogue and was accompanied by a dramatization of the stories. The plays concentrated on the two most important events – the Nativity and the Resurrection – and there is abundant evidence of how widespread they were and of the early incorporation of comic elements, which soon degenerated into farce, and even included burlesque sermons and bawdy songs. This led to criticism, so performances were banned from the churches and moved out into town squares and porticoes. A text of the *Partidas* of Alfonso X is often cited as showing how frequent these japes were – leaping and somersaults, dances, songs and parodies – which the clergy had to banish from their churches:

> ... first let us say that those who did them must be thrown out without ceremony, since God's church is made to pray in, and not to perform japes in ...

But a subsequent paragraph, on the other hand, clearly shows approval of the theatre:

> But there are dramas that clerics can perform, such as the birth of Our Saviour Jesus Christ, in which one sees how the angel came to the shepherds and how he told them Christ was born, as well as how the three Magi came to worship him. And his resurrection, which shows how he was crucified and raised on the third day. Such things as these, which move men to do good and to be devout in their faith, can be done ... But they must be done rightly and with great devotion ...

It has now been clearly established that medieval theatre had its origin in liturgical drama; it is important to stress the impact that these dramatizations had on the people of the Middle Ages – they were the only form of spectacle to which everyone had access.

1 The Christmas Cycle

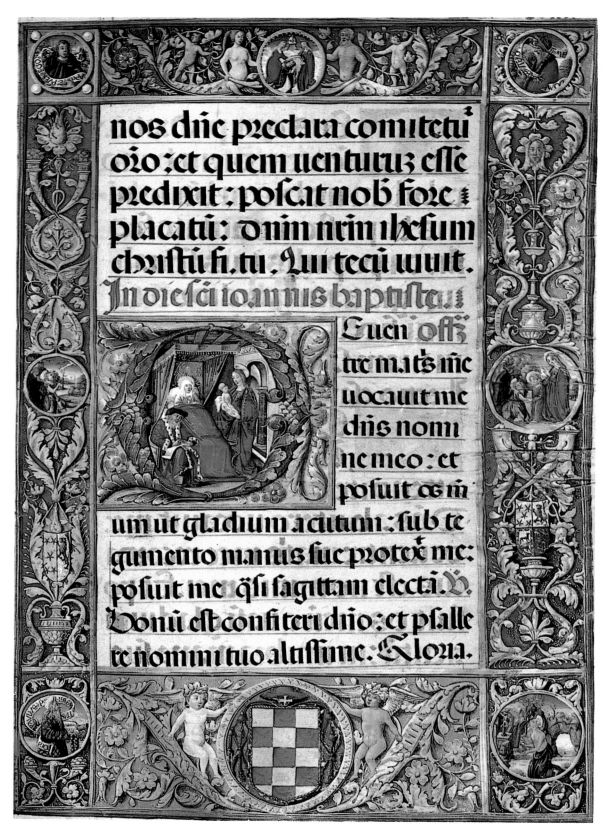

Misal rico of Cardinal Cisneros

This term, derived from the Latin *adventus*, 'coming', was applied originally not so much to the birth of Jesus as to his Second Coming, the Parousia, at the end of time. Later, from the eighth and ninth centuries, it came to designate the four weeks before Christmas, a time of preparation, but unlike Lent it did not have a penitential character, and throughout the period lauds were sung, the organ was played and the church was decorated with flowers.

During the Middle Ages, the feast of the fourth day in the week in which the Incarnation was celebrated was particularly solemn. On that day the gospel of St Luke was read, in which the Annunciation to Mary (*Missus est Gabriel angelus*) is narrated. In the Iberian peninsula this feast was celebrated on 18 December – not 25 March – from the time of the tenth Council of Toledo in 656. According to the Bayeux Ordinary, the gospel was read:

> at the pulpit, amidst lights, by a priest wearing white vestments and holding a palm branch in his hand.

The influence of this and other liturgical ceremonies at that period is shown by an unusual form of the iconography of the Annunciation, in which the angel offers the Virgin a palm branch, and the usual inscription, 'Ave Maria' is missing – this appears on the Clock Door of Toledo Cathedral, where we have accounts of liturgical plays from as far back as the thirteenth century.

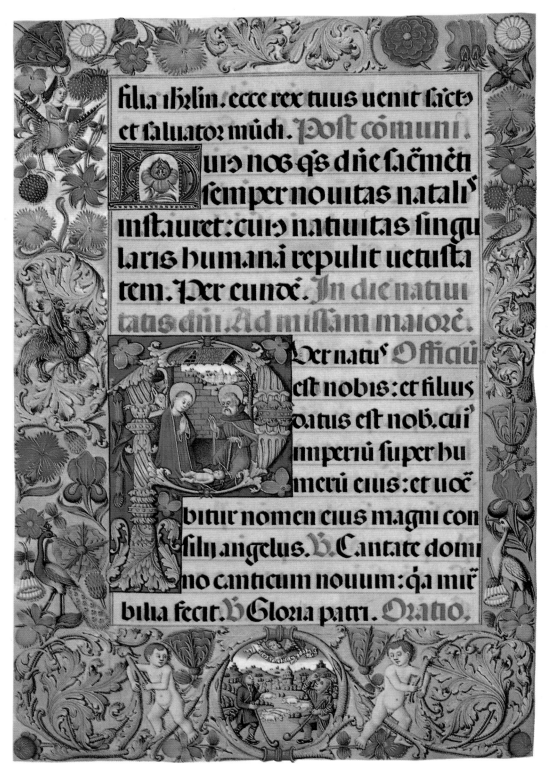

filia iħelm. ecce rex tuus uenit sactoz
et saluatoz mūch. Post cōmuni.
uis nos qs dñe sacmcti
semper nouitas natalis
instauret: cuis natiuitas singu
laris humanā repulit uetusta
tem. Per cundē. In die natiui
tatis dñi. Ad missam maiorē.
Per natus Officiū
est nobis: et filius
natus est nob. cui'
imperiū super hu
merū cius: et uoc̄
bitur nomen cius magni con
silu angelus. B. Cantate domi
no canticum nouum: ia mir
bilia fecit. B. Gloria patri. Oratio.

Misal rico of Cardinal Cisneros

The first record of the celebration of Christmas on 25 December comes from the year 336, in the *Depositio martyrum*, an outline of a liturgical calendar used in Rome, and it seems probable that the Church was substituting a celebration of the birth of Christ for the pagan feast celebrated on that day in honour of Mithras as 'Sol Invictus', the unconquered sun. As well as giving other examples of the Christianization of pagan feasts, commentaries by the earliest ecclesiastical writers also repeat the comparison of Christ with the sun, based not only on the cult of Mithras, but also directly as the 'Sol Novus' who is born on the winter solstice.

Misal rico of Cardinal Cisneros

To the office of the vigil – *ad galli cantum* – there was soon added a mass celebrated in St Peter's basilica in Rome; the feast acquired added importance when Sixtus III had the basilica of Santa Maria Maggiore rebuilt, with a special crypt, the Cripta del Presepe, to house the relics of the crib. The midnight mass was moved to Santa Maria Maggiore, leaving the great daytime celebration at St Peter's; later that too was moved to Santa Maria Maggiore.

As early as the eleventh century, according to a codex from Limoges which contains the text, a dramatization of the *Quem quaeritis in praesepe, pastores?* was performed during the Christmas mass. This would later be developed into the *Officium pastorum*, which is preserved in a version from the eleventh or twelfth century from Huesca cathedral. There is also a detailed description from the sixteenth century of a performance in Toledo cathedral; this would probably have been very similar to a performance of the thirteenth century, the date of the Castilian *coplas* of the text. One choir, made up of two cantors, asks the other choir, made up of acolytes dressed as shepherds, about the birth of Jesus. The latter answers by telling what they have seen in Bethlehem. The scene may very well have inspired the iconography of the Nativity scene that appears on the tympanum of the Clock Door at Toledo, which includes an early example of the shepherds playing musical instruments, just like the acolytes of the liturgical drama. It may also explain the usual iconography of the Nativity and the Annunciation to the Shepherds in illuminated missals, in the initial

letters and borders of the office of that day. Also in Toledo, according to a manuscript from the end of the fifteenth century, the so-called 'Song of the Sibyl' was played; this was a simplified version of the *Ordo prophetarum*, which, as the *General estoria* of Alfonso X explains, originated as the reading, during the Christmas matins, of a sermon falsely attributed to St Augustine (*Contra Judeos*), in which the prophets of the Old Testament and the pagan sibyl bear witness to the divinity of Christ. The sermon led to the liturgical play, and the church became the stage upon which appeared not only Isaiah, Jeremiah, Moses, Daniel and David, each reciting his piece, but also Virgil, Nebuchadnezzar and the Eritrean Sibyl, as shown in the relief on the church of St Martial in Limoges, dating from the second half of the eleventh century.

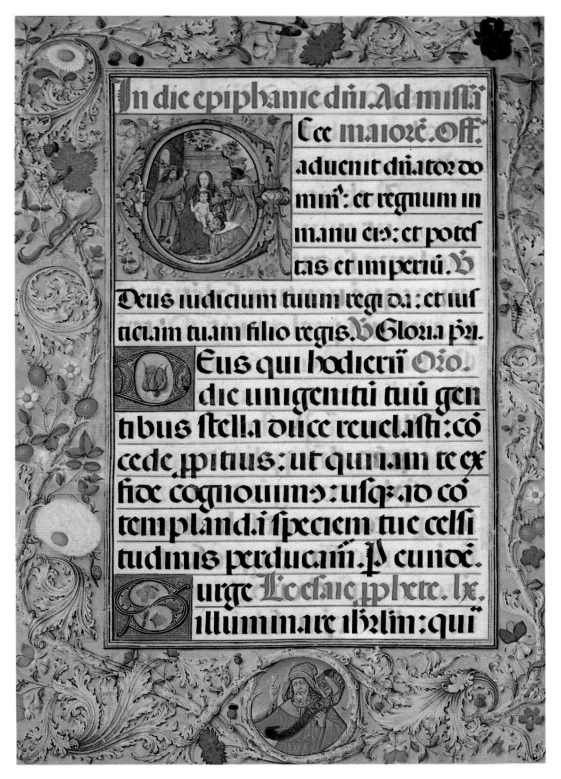

Misal rico of Cardinal Cisneros

231

In early liturgical calendars some of the saints' days are already estab-lished, among them the most popular ones, such as St Stephen's and the Holy Innocents'.

ST STEPHEN'S The cult of St Stephen spread quickly throughout the Church after his relics were discovered on 5 December 415, at Caphargamala near Jerusalem; They were transferred to a martyrium, as recounted in great detail in the *Legenda aurea* by Jacobus de Voragine. In the Middle Ages, Stephen's feast day, 26 December, was considered to be special to deacons, and on that day it was the deacons who presided over the choir and chanted the epistle, the alleluia and the gradual of the mass.

HOLY INNOCENTS' The Holy Innocents are commemorated on 28 December. The tomb of the Innocents in Bethlehem does not seem to have been the object of particular devotion in the first centuries of the Christian era. In the early Middle Ages, however, the day became the special feast of the choirboys and acolytes. On that day, in numerous churches in France, Germany and Italy, the canons gave up their places so that the choirboys or acolytes could preside over the liturgical service (apart from the mass), directed by their leader wearing the appropriate insignia. In some places a 'bishop' was chosen from among them – the *episcopellus* – who, dressed in pontifical vestments with mitre and crosier, sat in the bishop's chair and gave the solemn blessing. This 'Feast of the Little Bishop' was celebrated in various cathedrals in Spain, according to Caro Baroja; he also records that in Seville cathedral in 1512 the ciborium collapsed on Holy Innocents' day, and this was interpreted as a sign of divine displeasure at the irreverent behaviour of the 'little bishop' and his companions in the church. Even so, the feast continued to be celebrated there until 1563, when it was banned from the cathedral.

However, the feasts that relate to the life of Jesus – the Circumcision and Epiphany – are naturally the most important ones.

THE CIRCUMCISION The Circumcision was established on 1 January because that is the eighth day after Christmas. In the pagan world the Roman festival of the Saturnalia took place at the new year, and this was a time of revelry and licence, in which Christians also participated, as Tertullian and St Augustine relate. Because of this, the Christian Church decided that penitential litanies should be said during the first three days of January, and at the fourth

Council of Toledo a rigorous fast similar to the Lenten one was established. The expiatory character disappeared during the sixth to eighth centuries, for the Church decided that it would be more effective to incorporate 1 January as a Christian feast, at first a feast in honour of the virginity of Mary, but this was gradually replaced by the feast of the Circumcision, which was celebrated in Spain as early as the sixth century. It quickly spread to France, but there is no mention of it in Rome before the eleventh century.

The Epiphany, on the other hand, is one of the most ancient liturgical feasts. Of eastern origin, as its Greek name indicates – *Epiphania* or *Theophania* – the first record that we have of it is from the beginning of the third century, when Clement of Alexandria says that on that day, 6 January, the Basilidians, a Gnostic sect, commemorated the Adoration of the Magi and the Baptism of Christ; it is probable that it was also celebrated in some eastern churches. It was known in the West by the middle of the fourth century, and at the Council of Zaragoza in the year 380 it was recognized as a feast day, although in the West it was not the Baptism which was celebrated so much as the manifestation of Jesus to the Wise Men as king and lord of all nations. In the West, from the eighth century on, the Baptism was celebrated on the first Sunday after Epiphany, although the rite of the blessing of the water is preserved in the mass of the Epiphany.

As in the celebration of Christmas, the liturgy of the Epiphany included a night vigil and a solemn mass, in which there was a dramatization of the *Ordo stellae*, a retelling of the apparition of the star to the Wise Men, of their journey and their offering of gifts. This theme, a very popular one in Christian iconography, soon became an inspiration for paraliturgical theatre, and we have a Spanish text of one of these dramas, the *Representación o Auto de los Reyes Magos*, from the mid-twelfth century, the first extant theatre piece in a Romance language.

Misal rico of Cardinal Cisneros

233

At the beginning of January, but not on a set date, two of the most popular feasts of the Middle Ages took place: the *Festum asinorum* (Feast of the Donkey), and the *Festum stultorum* (Feast of Fools); these were part of the Christian liturgy, in spite of their essentially profane character. It is easy to deduce that the dances and games that took place inside churches on these occasions soon acquired a carnival aspect, and despite repeated prohibitions in church councils they lasted well into the sixteenth century.

The Feast of the Donkey originated, it seems, in the dramatization of the *Ordo prophetarum* or 'Drama of the Prophets', where Barlaam appears riding on a donkey. In the cathedral of Sens it came to have its own liturgy composed by Bishop Pierre de Corbeil in the first half of the

Misal rico of Cardinal Cisneros

thirteenth century, and in Beauvais it was incorporated into the celebration of the Flight into Egypt on 16 January. On that day, a richly harnessed donkey, upon which a baby girl was placed, went in procession from the cathedral to the church of St Stephen, where the animal, with the baby riding it, assisted at the mass. The other event, the Feast of Fools, seems to have been inspired by the festival dedicated to acolytes and choirboys on Holy Innocents' Day. It was dedicated to subdeacons, who also elected their 'little bishop', parodying the bishop's liturgical functions; clerics and priests also participated.

The Christmas cycle ended on 2 February, which is dedicated to the Presentation in the Temple and the Purification of the Virgin, and is also known as Candlemas. The first reference to the liturgical celebration of the feast appears in the *Pelegrinatio* of the nun Egeria, who was present at it in Jerusalem in 381. Originally it commemorated only the Presentation of Jesus in the Temple, which according to Hebrew law had to be done within forty days after birth. This accounts for the fact that from the first the feast was set on 2 February; there is no allusion to processions with lighted candles, however, until the sixth century. Certain Christian authors, among them the Venerable Bede, have explained this celebration as the attempt to set up a Christian ceremony in opposition to the processions of the Roman Lupercalia, although this does not seem particularly convincing, for the Lupercalia was celebrated on 15 January and its rites seem to have nothing in common with Candlemas. Moreover, the mass and office on 2 February celebrate principally the Presentation of Jesus in the Temple and his encounter with Simeon, the Purification of the Virgin being merely mentioned, though this evidently acquired a central focus when the procession was incorporated. In it, the candles that the faithful carried were lit from a special candle and kept, for after being blessed they were believed to be particularly efficacious in epidemics, in difficulties in childbirth, and in storms. In Spanish liturgical calendars the feast does not appear until the eleventh century, but the procession must have been popular throughout the West by the twelfth century, judging by the writings of Honorius of Autun, and by its influence on the iconography of the period.

THE PURIFICATION OF THE VIRGIN

235

2. THE EASTER CYCLE

LENT

This is a time of penitence in preparation for Easter, and it is divided into three pre-Lenten weeks, Lent proper and Holy Week.

The three pre-Lenten weeks are known as Septuagesima, Sexagesima and Quinquagesima, from their relationship to Quadragesima, or the first week of Lent; these three weeks were added at a later date to the Lenten fast and penance, following the usual practice of the monks. The first to be added, and the closest to Lent, was Quinquagesima, instituted under Pope Hilary (461-8), and the last, Septuagesima, had come into existence by the end of the sixth century. During this period, beginning with Septuagesima, readings are taken from the Old Testament, starting with Genesis.

The real preparation for Easter is Lent, the forty days leading up to Easter, in commemoration of the forty days of fasting of Moses and Elijah and, most of all, of Christ's forty days of fasting in the desert. Thus, fasting was from the first associated with Lent. Initially, only one meal was taken, late in the afternoon at the hour of Vespers; from the thirteenth and fourteenth centuries on it was moved to midday. The *Apostolic Constitutions* laid down that food during Lent should consist only of bread, legumes, salt and water; later milk, cheese, eggs, fish and wine were also allowed. On the first day of Lent the faithful received a sprinkling of ashes on their foreheads, and so the day is called Ash Wednesday; normally people went to confession on that day in order to purify the soul. Every form of liturgical feast was prohibited throughout the period; at the end of Lent, during Passion Week, all crosses and images in churches were covered as a sign of mourning.

HOLY WEEK

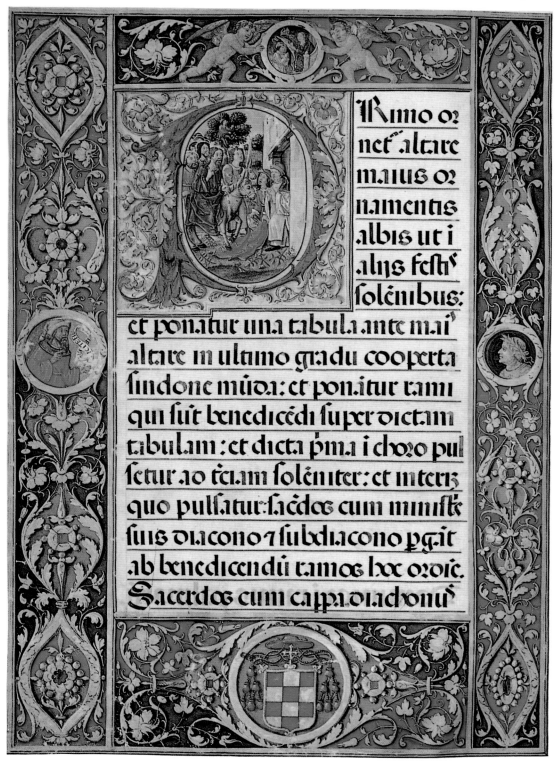

Rimo or
net altare
maius or
namentis
albis ut i
alijs festi
solénibus:
et ponatur una tabula ante mai'
altare in ultimo gradu cooperta
sindone müoa: et ponatur rami
qui sut benedicédi super oictam
tabulam: et dicta pm̃a i choro pul
setur ao téram solém iter: et interz
quo pulsatur: facéoes cum minist̃
suis oiacono ⁊ subdiacono pgit
ab benedicendü ramos hoc oroíc.
Sacerdos cum cappa oiachonus

Misal rico of Cardinal Cisneros

239

This is the week that immediately precedes Easter and is therefore dedicated to commemorating the passion and death of Christ; the ceremonies associated with Holy Week have been in existence since the fourth century.

PALM SUNDAY Holy Week began with the *Dominica palmorum* or Palm Sunday, a name derived from the procession with palm branches commemorating the entry of Christ into Jerusalem, so fulfilling the prophecy of Zechariah (ix,9). An exceptional testimony to its development at the end of the fourth century comes to us from the account of the nun Egeria, who went on a pilgrimage to the Holy Land and was present at the ceremony in Jerusalem:

> On the Mount of Olives the corresponding gospel text is read... And at that point the bishop and all the people stand and from the highest point of the Mount of Olives the whole way is done on foot. All the people go before the bishop singing hymns and antiphons, always responding, 'Blessed is he who comes in the name of the Lord.' And all the little children from those places, even those who are too young to walk and have to be carried in the arms of their parents, carry branches, some of them palms and others olives; and the bishop is carried in the same way as was the Lord.

The participation of the whole population, led by the bishop and the clergy, was the custom during the Middle Ages, according to numerous Ordinaries and Rituals; often the blessing of the branches and the adoration of the Cross was included in the ceremony.

In southern Germany and Alsace, ever since the time of St Ulrick, bishop of Augusta at the end of the tenth century, the so-called 'Donkey of the Palm' was carried in the procession – a wooden donkey with the figure of Christ astride it, which was later exhibited in the church. In medieval Rituals this Sunday was sometimes known as *Pascua floridum* or *Dies floridum* because, as well as palm and olive branches, flowers were also blessed, which must surely be a reminiscence of the pagan feasts of spring.

240

HOLY THURSDAY The commemoration of the passion and death of Christ continued on Holy Thursday, or *feria quinta in Coena Domini*, the commemoration of the Last Supper, and thus the Institution of the Eucharist, to which are added the Agony in the Garden and Judas' betrayal. The liturgy began with the

Misal rico of Cardinal Cisneros

Tenebrae Matins, in which a special triangular candlestick was used, which held fifteen candles – these were put out one by one at the end of each psalm, finishing the ceremony with all the candles but one extinguished in memory of Christ's suffering.

Later, during mass, came the consecration of the oils and the washing of feet *ad mandatum*, the bishop washing the feet of twelve poor people in imitation of Christ washing the feet of the disciples. This ceremony was very common in the Church from the earliest times, and was considered mandatory at the seventeenth Council of Toledo in 694.

The account of the nun Egeria is especially significant for understanding the participation of the faithful in these ceremonies. She attended in the celebrations in Jerusalem during her visit in 381-4, and here she refers to the prayers on the Mount of Olives and Jesus' arrest:

> Upon coming to Gethsemane, an appropriate prayer is said, together with a hymn; then the text of the gospel where the Lord was arrested is read. After this text has been read, the whole population breaks forth in sobs, wails and weeping, and sometimes these cries of the whole population can be heard in the city. After-

241

wards, everyone goes to the city on foot singing hymns; they arrive at the gate at the hour in which a man can barely distinguish himself from another, and from there all go into the midst of the city, with no one missing: old and young, rich and poor, all are present.

Then follows the account of the Good Friday liturgy, in which: 'before sundown, all promptly go to Zion to pray before the column at which the Lord was scourged'.

Later, the Adoration of the Cross takes place:

> the silver reliquary plated with gold is taken out in which the holy wood of the cross is kept. It is then opened and [the contents] are removed, and both the wood of the cross and the inscription are placed on the table...and the whole people comes forward one by one, both the faithful and catechumens, and bowing before the table they kiss the holy wood and pass by.

242

This ceremony was soon imitated in many eastern and western

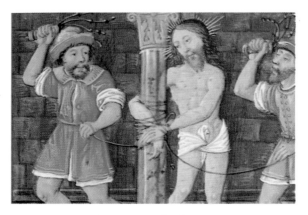

Misal rico of Cardinal Cisneros

churches, in many of which a relic of the True Cross was preserved. This rite was the most important one in the Good Friday liturgy; to it were added the uncovering and exposition of the Cross with a triple prostration and the dialogue chant of the *Populus meus*, the *Improperios* and the Byzantine *Trisagion*, which were incorporated into the Roman liturgy between the ninth and eleventh centuries.

Misal rico of Cardinal Cisneros

EASTER

The celebration of Easter began (as is usual in the liturgy) with a night vigil, in which were included the blessing of the new flame, necessary for lighting the candle, the blessing of the five grains of incense, necessary for making the sign of the Cross over the candle and finally the solemn blessing of the Pascal Candle, which from the thirteenth century sometimes consisted of three candles – *candela trium ramorum*

Misal rico of Cardinal Cisneros

244

– that were lit one after the other; this has been interpreted in various ways, as a symbol of the Trinity or as a reference to the three Marys at the sepulchre. The blessing followed a rite attributed to St Augustine, the *Laus cerei*, the *Praeconium paschale*, or the *Exultet*, celebrating the victory of Christ over death and darkness, which included a hymn in praise of the bees which had made the wax of the candle and whose chastity recalls the virgin birth of Christ. A custom widespread in the Middle Ages consisted of writing on the candle, or on a tablet hanging from it, the current year and the dates of the most important movable feasts; this meant that the candle often had to be extremely large, almost a column. It was placed in a special candlestick, and some medieval examples of these are preserved in Italy; in Rome, Salerno, Capua, Palermo, Benavento and elsewhere.

In the early Church all candidates for baptism were baptized at Easter or Pentecost and during the mass the general communion of the faithful took place. However, other ceremonies had more impact on the popular development of the feast. Thus, in the Matins three responses were sung recalling the visit of the three holy women to the sepulchre, the search for Christ's body and the announcement by the angel of the Resurrection. These three episodes were the origin of the most ancient liturgical play known,

Misal rico of Cardinal Cisneros

the so-called *Quem quaeritis in sepulcro?;* later it developed into the *Visitatio sepulchri,* which contains the conversation between the women who go to anoint Christ's body and the angel who receives them seated upon the empty tomb.

In its shortest form, the *Quem quaeritis in sepulchro?* appears in a manuscript at St Martial in Limoges from *circa* 933, and there is evidence that it was sung and dramatized in the liturgy of Easter Sunday from the end of the tenth century. In Spain, an example of the *Visitatio sepulchri*

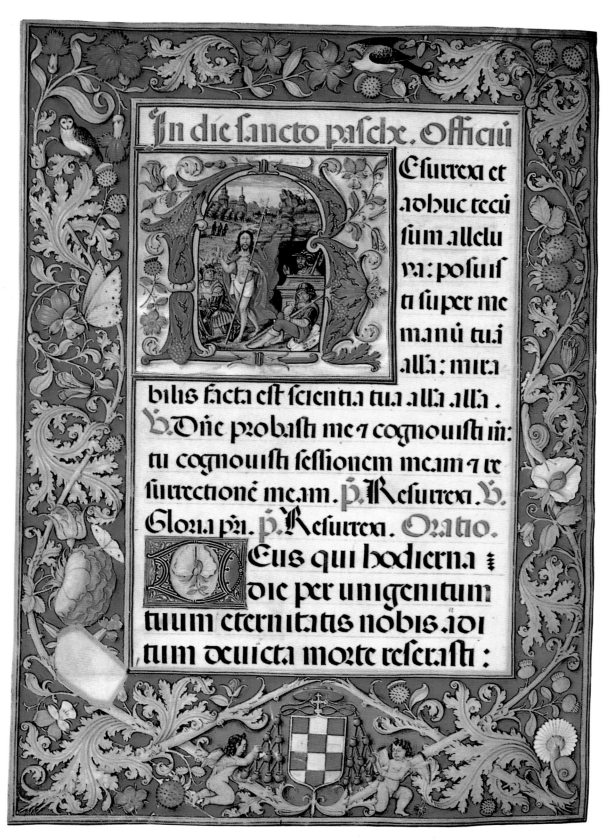

Misal rico of Cardinal Cisneros

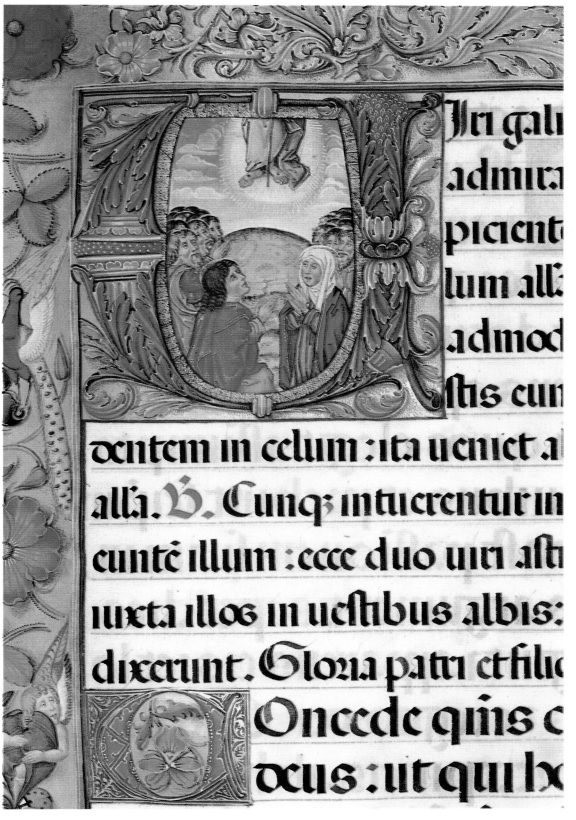

Jri galī
admira
picient
lum all.
admod
stis cur
dentem in celum : ita ueniet a
allā. V. Cunq; intuerentur in
cunte illum : ecce duo uiri asti
iuxta illos in uestibus albis :
dixerunt. Gloria patri et filio
Oncede quis o
deus : ut qui he

247

Misal rico of Cardinal Cisneros

was included in a breviary of the end of the eleventh century from the monastery of Silos, now in the British Museum, and another text, also from the end of the eleventh century, has been preserved in a codex from Ripoll. A later text, from the end of the twelfth century, is contained in the *Codex Calixtinus*. It is known that the play was put on at the end of the thirteenth century in the cathedral of Vich, and in the fourteenth century in the monastery of Santa María de Estany. Its influence in the iconography of the era has been pointed out by Emile Mâle, and extends even to comic scenes, such as that of the Marys buying ointments to anoint the body of Christ – inspired directly by the text – which appears on Romanesque capitals in the south of France.

THE ASCENSION In the days following Easter, the Ascension and Pentecost, the feast that ends the Easter cycle, are celebrated. It seems that originally both were commemorated on the same day, as in the account of the nun Egeria of her visit to Jerusalem in 381, but from the fifth century the Ascension begins to acquire its own liturgy. In it was included the ancient Roman custom of the blessing of beans, representing, as it were, the first of the new fruit, but this rite disappeared during the medieval centuries.

PENTECOST Pentecost coincides with the so-called 'Feast of Weeks' of Exodus xxxiv,22, which was celebrated seven weeks after Easter, giving thanks to God for the wheat harvest, but in the Christian era it came to commemorate the apostles receiving the gifts of the Holy Spirit, so launching the Church's mission in the world. The Jewish origin of the festival explains why it is mentioned as early as the beginning of the second century, although it only began to acquire importance in the fourth, when baptism for those who were not able to receive it at Easter was incorporated into the night vigil. In the middle of the ninth century the hymn *Veni, Creator Spiritus* was introduced; it was sung at the third hour after sunrise, and was accompanied in many churches in France and Italy by a rain of roses, flowers and even small pieces of cloth set aflame, in imitation of the tongues of fire that descended upon the apostles.

248

Misal rico of Cardinal Cisneros

249

THE PERIOD BETWEEN
PENTECOST AND ADVENT

Misal rico of Cardinal Cisneros

Misal rico of Cardinal Cisneros

This was the last to take shape; in it important feasts for the Church were established during the whole of the Middle Ages.

TRINITY SUNDAY AND THE ASSUMPTION

Examples of feasts occurring between Pentecost and Advent are Trinity Sunday, instituted and extended to the whole Church only in 1334 by John XXII, or certain feasts in honour of the Virgin, such as the Assumption on 15 August, established at the beginning of the sixth century, or her birth, 8 September, not established until the seventh century.

Also during this period there are feast days of saints that were popular in the Middle Ages, such as Sts Peter and Paul on 29 June, St Michael on 29 September and the birth of St John the Baptist on 24 June.

CORPUS CHRISTI

One of the most popular festivals was the feast of Corpus Christi, on the Thursday after Trinity Sunday, celebrated as early as the year 1000; it achieved widespread popularity in the thirteenth century, after the famous miracle of Bolsena in 1264. Soon processions were introduced, and there are references to them in Cologne in 1279, at Würzburg in 1298 and somewhat later in 1323 at Paris and 1350 at Rome.

251

The Tradition of the Medieval Calendar

Sefer Evronot, by Pinhas ben Avraham of
Halberstadt, 1716.
Jerusalem, Jewish National and
University Library

The months of the year, from top to bottom

JANUARIUS

FEBRUARIUS

MARTIUS

APRIL

MAIUS

JULIUS

JULIUS

AUGUSTUS

SEPTEMBER

OCTOBER

NOVEMBER

DECEMBER

SPRING

The month of April. Making butter

Medieval manuscripts occasionally show cheese-making, but in later manuscripts it became more usual to illustrate the production of butter, another task given to women (in this case exclusively).

SUMMER
The month of July. Reaping barley
The fact that both reaping with scythes and threshing are shown indicates that this is the harvesting of barley, which takes place rather earlier than the wheat harvest in northern Europe.

257

AUTUMN

The month of October. The vintage

Both men and women are involved in the production of wine: preparing the casks and barrels, gathering the grapes, carrying the baskets of grapes to the press and treading the grapes.

WINTER

The month of January. The traditional medieval scene

As late as the eighteenth century, the winter period is still represented by the traditional medieval subjects for the season: fire and food. The setting has changed, as has the clothing, but the stove still provides warmth in the cold weather and the table is laid ready for a meal.

The connection between the calendar and agricultural tasks originated in Roman cycles and was definitively established in medieval iconographic schemes. Several centuries later, in the eighteenth century, traces of the tradition can still be perceived in, for example, the calendar in the manuscript *Sefer Evronot*, the work of Pinhas ben Avraham of Halberstadt, dated 1716 (Jerusalem, Jewish National and University Library). In it, certain details reflect the period: the peasant, who looks quite prosperous, is wearing hat, coat, stockings and boots at his work in the fields, and he may smoke a pipe or warm himself at a stove; the presence of women in various scenes; the interest in landscape; birds or fruit on the trees emphasizing the change of seasons.

Nevertheless, the medieval tradition persists, with the agricultural tasks characterisizing each of the months, the majority repeating the labours or occupations shown in the medieval cycles.

JANUARY

This scene is set in a prosperous household. It shows a comfortable room warmed by a central European type of stove, replacing the traditional illustration of an open fire. It also contains a reference to the winter banquet, in the table in the background set with food, bread and a pitcher of beer. A man, standing, holds his hands close to the stove in order to warm himself, the usual attitude of the personification of January; the figure of the two-headed Janus is alluded to in his unusual stance, his profile accentuated by the backwards turn of his head. Thus in the *Januarius* of the eighteenth century, the banquet and the fire still play their part.

FEBRUARY

The traditional depiction of March, pruning the vines, has been moved to February, and is shown alongside the work of tree pruning, also carried out at this time. In both scenes, the peasant is dressed in an elegant coat, stockings and high boots, according to the fashion of the period, and wears a small hat with a brim, more suited to a stroll than to work in the fields. A knife is used for pruning the vines, and an axe for cutting off the dead branches. The plants that appear in the background suggest the arrival of spring, as do the birds, especially the one flying above, which may be a stork.

MARCH

Once again we have a double scene, divided by an almond tree in flower in the centre – again a reference to the beginning of spring. The good weather also explains why the left-hand figure is in his shirt-sleeves. He is taking a break from his work, his foot resting on a spade or hoe, while he smokes a pipe, a habit which spread through Europe from the seventeenth century on. He has probably been digging in preparation for transplanting as seems to be indicated by the green plants lined up in furrows and the jugs used for watering them in, shown in the background. In contrast, the figure on the right is still warmly dressed, since sowing requires less effort – he is simply broadcasting the seeds that he carries in his apron. The seeds themselves are shown lying in the ploughed furrows.

APRIL

April is identified here with the making of butter, a task which, like cheese-making, was most frequently depicted in fifteenth-century miniatures, when women were more often shown taking part in agricultural work. Outdoors, beside the farmhouse, two women are busy beating the cream in butter churns, which in the Middle Ages were made of wood, with staves and hoops like casks and barrels, but taller and narrower, and tapering towards the top. The handle of the agitator protrudes through the lid. The minute detail allows us to distinguish an early stage of the process, on the right, where the woman is vigorously dashing the agitator up and down, and a later phase, where the woman on the left takes out the solid white curds that can be seen at the top of the churn. Also connected with women's work is the depiction in the upper part of the scene of a garden with vegetables and flowers – frequently the women's responsibility in the medieval peasant economy.

MAY

Here the spring outing and the hunt, both pursuits of the nobility, have been amalgamated. The man is wearing ordinary eighteenth-century dress, but in addition he has a tall hat adorned with a leafy branch – a traditional motif of spring – and a red sash, and other indications of high status, such as the star-shaped spur and the richly patterned fabric of the fringed saddle-cloth. The horse is trotting along and the rider, although he holds a small horn to his lips, seems to ignore the dogs pursuing a boar beside him. The boar is lured by bait (the only feasible interpretation of the strange humanoid figures on the tree at the left) into the trap made of nets held up by posts, where it is cornered. This type of hunting, common in the Roman era, is rarely shown in medieval manuscripts, for the use of traps was then deemed unworthy of a proper huntsman. Gaston Phébus writes:

> For my taste, one should not even mention it, or teach hunting at all, unless it be done with nobility and courtesy, and for enjoyment, and there would be more animals if they were not killed by bad methods … So, as I said at the beginning of my book that good huntsmen live long and happy lives and go to Heaven when they die, I want to teach everyone to be huntsmen of one kind or another. I am sure that unless a man is a good huntsman he will not enter paradise, but I believe that a huntsman of the other type, though he will not be at the centre of paradise, will at least be on the outskirts of it …

This reasoning justifies the description in the text of the use of traps, pens, nets, bait and pits, even though they were considered unethical by the nobility in the Middle Ages.

264

JUNE

With the arrival of summer the heat begins to become oppressive and the woman seeks the shade of a tree while she shears a sheep. At her side, a large basket holds the shorn fleece. Much of the scene is taken up by two solid buildings with steeply sloping roofs which are covered with shingles, as was usual in central and northern Europe. The larger size of the door and windows of the building on the left lead us to surmise that it is a barn and that the one on the right houses the living quarters.

JULY

A reaping scene; the use of the scythe, and the timing of the harvest in northern Europe, might seem to indicate that this is a haymaking scene, which would explain the green colour of parts of the field. However, the carefully drawn stems of corn and fact that it is tied up in sheaves suggests that it is actually a depiction of barley reaping, which occurs somewhat earlier than the wheat harvest. On the left-hand side, at the top, a well-dressed man in a three-cornered hat typical of the eighteenth century is pensively contemplating the scene and holding his scythe. The other figures, including a woman who is raking the straw into piles, are hard at work.

AUGUST

A peasant is reaping the wheat with a sickle. In the foreground are two sheaves ready to be carried away by the woman who appears unobtrusively in the lower right-hand corner. The true subject of this scene, however, is the landscape itself. A wide field of wheat takes up half the picture, the golden colour contrasting with the fresh green of the trees, which are laden with fruit. The intense heat is indicated by the ripe sheaves, the rolled-up sleeves of the reaper and the wide-brimmed hat protecting him from the rays of the sun.

265

SEPTEMBER

A flock of migratory birds in the upper right-hand corner marks the end of summer and the row of stooks in the background acts as a reminder of the recent harvest. The earth is being ploughed ready for sowing next year's cereal; one man leads the horse that pulls the plough, while the other guides the ploughshare along the furrow and at the same time sows the seed with his left hand.

OCTOBER

The traditional vintage scene is here focused on the different stages of wine-making. In the upper part, a man prepares the vats and barrels, with the vineyard in the background; most of the grapes have been picked but at the extreme left two vines still bear bunches of grapes. Grapes fill the large basket at the foot. In the foreground, a peasant empties his basket into a barrel, while another with a pannier on his back crushes the grapes in a barrel with a shovel. In the centre is a man treading the grapes as a woman tips them in. As in the other scenes, the dress of the figures is curious, particularly that of the man treading the grapes, who is wearing a buttoned overcoat and a wide-brimmed hat.

NOVEMBER

In this cycle women as well as men are shown at work, and this explains the inclusion of this untraditional scene, which has no precedent in medieval calendars. Weaving and sewing and the care of farm animals, all women's work, were not seasonal tasks and so they cannot be associated with a particular month. However, this peaceful scene in the farmyard, with the hen and her chicks pecking at seed and the rooster pecking at a bush, is well suited to November, the end of autumn.

DECEMBER

Once again, the landscape has a central role; the ground is covered with fallen leaves and the branches are bare. Two figures, walking in oppposite directions and apparently ignoring each other, are using poles to gather fruit - probably nuts - which one of them carries in a bag on his back. He is dressed in an overcoat or frock-coat, longer than usual in order to protect himself from the cold; clouds of smoke are issuing from his pipe.

267

BIBLIOGRAPHY

Camps i Soria, J., *El claustre de la catedral de Tarragona: escultura de l'ala meridional*, Barcelona, 1988

Capelli, G., *I mesi Antelamici nel Battistero di Parma*, Parma, 1973

Caro Baroja, J., *Tecnología popular española*, Madrid, 1983; in particular, 'Los menologios y el año agrícola', pp. 39-110, and 'Los arados españoles. Sus tipos y repartición', pp. 509-97

Castelnovo, E., *Il ciclo dei mesi di Torre Aquila a Trento*, Trento, 1987

Castiñeiras, M.A., 'Gennaio e Giano bifronte: dalle "anni januae" all'interno domestico (secoli XII-XIII)', *Prospectiva*, 66 (1992), pp. 53-63

— 'Algunas peculiaridades iconográficas del calendario medieval hispano: las escenas de trilla y labranza (ss. XI-XIV)', *Archivo Español de Arte*, 261 (1993), pp. 57-70

Cohen, S., 'The Romanesque Zodiac: Its Symbolic Function on the Church Façade', *Arte Medievale*, IV (1990), pp. 43-4

Domínguez Rodríguez, A., 'Iconografía de los signos del Zodíaco en seis Libros de Horas de la Biblioteca Nacional', *Revista de la Universidad Complutense*, XXII, 85 (1974), pp. 26-80

Frugoni, C., 'Chiesa e lavoro agricolo nei testi e nelle immagini dall'età tardoantica all'età romanica', *in Medioevo rurale. Sulle tracce della civiltà contadina*, Bologna, 1980, pp. 321-41

Herrera Casado, A., 'El calendario románico de Beleña de Sorbe (Guadalajara)', *Traza y Baza*, 5 (1974), pp. 31-40

Le Senecal, J. 'Les occupations des mois dans l'iconographie du Moyen Age', *Bulletin de la Société des Antiquaires de Normandie*, XXXV (1921-23), p. 1-131

Levi, D., 'The Allegories of the Months in Classical Art', *Art Bulletin*, 23 (1941), pp. 251-91

Longnon, J., and Cazelles, R., *Les Très Riches Heures du duc de Berry*, Paris, 1970

Mane, P., *Calendriers et techniques agricoles (France et Italie XIIme - XIIIme siècles)*, Paris, 1983

— 'Comparaison des thèmes iconographiques des calendriers monumentaux et enluminés en France aux XIIme et XIIIme siècles', *Cahiers de Civilisation Médiévale*, XXIX (1986), pp. 257-64

Moralejo Alvarez, S., 'Pour l'interpretation iconographique du Portail de l'Agneau à Saint-Isidore de León: les signes du Zodiaque', *Cahiers de Saint Michel de Cuxá*, 8 (1977), pp. 137-73

Palol, P. de, *El tapis de la Creació de la catedral de Girona*, Barcelona, 1986

Riguetti, M., *Historia de la Liturgia*, I, Madrid, 1955

Ruiz Montejo, I., 'El calendario de Beleña de Sorbe', *Anales de Historia del Arte de la Universidad Complutense*, 4 (1994), pp. 491-503

Schapiro, M., 'The Carolingian Copy of the Calendar of 354', *Art Bulletin*, XXII (1940), pp. 270-72

Schumann, R., 'Il re nel ciclo dell'anno del Battistero di Parma', *Archivio storico per le province parmensi*, 4» serie, XXIV (1972), pp. 129-37

Stern, H., *Le caelndrier de 354. Etude sur son texte et sur ses illustrations*, Paris, 1953

— 'Poésies et representations carolingiennes et byzantines des mois', *Revue Archéologique*, XLIV (1955), pp. 141-86

— 'Le zodiaque de Beth-Alpha', *L'Oeil*, September 1956, pp. 15-19

Taralon, J., 'Les peintures murales nouvellement découvertes de l'église de Pritz (Mayenne)', *Monuments et Mémoires Fondation Eugène Piot*, LIV (1965), pp. 61-7

Webster, J.C., *The Labours of the Months in Antique and Medieval Art, to the End of the Twelfth Century*, Princeton, 1938

Manuscripts referred to in the text

Astrological Calendar and Martyrology of Swabia (Stuttgart, Württembergische Landesbibliothek, cod. hist.415)

Bedford Hours (London, British Museum, ms. Add. 18850)

Breviari d'amor (Madrid, Biblioteca National, Res. 203)

Calendar of St Mesmin (Rome, Vatican Library, Vat. Reg. lat.1263)

Catalogue of the Fixed Stars, al-Sufi (Oxford, Bodleian Library, ms. Marsh 144)

Chronograph of Philocalus of 354 (copies from the fifteenth and seventeenth century – Vienna, Österreichische Nationalbibliotek, cod. 3416, and Rome, Vatican Library, Bib. Apostolica, MS Barb. lat. 2154)

Fulda Calendar (Berlin, Bibliothek National, ms. Theol. lat. f.192)

Martyrology of Wandalbert of Prüm (Rome, Vatican Library, Vat. Reg. lat. 438)

Missal of Archbishop Alonso Carrillo de Acuña (Toledo, Cathedral Chapter Library, ms. Res. 1)

Missal of the Confraternity of the Holy Cross, Avignon (Madrid, Biblioteca Nacional)

Sefer Evronot, Pinhas ben Avraham of Halberstadt (Jerusalem, Jewish National and University Library)

Les Très Riches Heures du Duc de Berry (Chantilly, Musée Condé)

Vienna Calendar (Vienna, Österreichische Nationalbibliothek, cod.387, fol.90 v)